# HUDSON MACK

# HUDSON MACK

## UNSINKABLE ANCHOR

## Hudson Mack

HARBOUR PUBLISHING

Harbour Publishing Co. Ltd.
P.O. Box 219, Madeira Park, BC, V0N 2H0
www.harbourpublishing.com

Photos courtesy of the author's collection except where otherwise noted
Edited by Derek Fairbridge
Text design by Mary White
Printed and bound in Canada
Printed on 100% post-consumer waste
Index by Brianna Cerkiewicz

Harbour Publishing acknowledges the support of the Canada Council for the
Arts, which last year invested $157 million to bring the arts to Canadians
throughout the country. We also gratefully acknowledge financial support
from the Government of Canada through the Canada Book Fund and from
the Province of British Columbia through the BC Arts Council and the Book
Publishing Tax Credit.

Cataloguing data available from Library and Archives Canada
ISBN 978-1-55017-720-6 (cloth)
ISBN 978-1-55017-721-3 (ebook)

*Dedicated to my family*

# Contents

# 1

# The End

This is the end.

Well, maybe not the way Jim Morrison meant. And, oddly enough, when it comes, the end isn't a big surprise to me. Actually, I think I saw it coming. And it's not really *the end*, of course. Just the end of "this." Whatever "this" is—or was. I had expected it to land like a punch in the gut. A kick in the teeth. Oddly enough, it didn't. Maybe it will yet. But it hasn't happened so far, and in the meantime I'm not holding my breath.

I first see the email as I'm scanning the inbox on my iPhone just after 8:00 AM in the midst of my usual routine. It's a sunny Thursday in February 2014, five days before my fifty-fourth birthday. I am cleaning up after making breakfast for our youngest son, Sheldon, a seventeen-year-old high school senior with little else on his mind but playing football in the fall on a varsity scholarship for the University of British Columbia.

If I make a face when I see the email, he doesn't notice; he is oblivious, as I read and then reread the words on my phone. His lunch is packed. It's the usual, though I agonize each morning to make something different and interesting. His older brother and sister are still asleep. His mother is still in bed, but awake with a freshly delivered cup of coffee, her laptop, phone and the morning's *Victoria Times Colonist*. All part of our morning routine. Everything normal so far. Except the email.

Patty will stew if I tell her about the email, I think. No disrespect to stewing, but that would be putting it mildly. There isn't much to read between the lines of the message even if I'd gone looking. So there is no point telling her, at least not yet. Don't meet trouble halfway, I always say.

Sheldon asks to take the car to school that day. I'm not sure why he wants or needs it, if there even is a reason, but I'm happy to oblige. It means taking the bus to work at CTV Vancouver Island, but that isn't unusual for me. Nor is it much of a hardship. The bus picks me up at a stop a few doors from our home and just around the corner, and less than fifteen minutes later, BC Transit's #14 spits me out on a downtown Victoria curb just a couple of blocks from the television station. Sometimes other passengers stare at me in recognition (*Isn't that the guy from . . .*), but I like riding the bus to work. Or did.

I am a creature of habit. I usually eat—or ate—the same food every day: meals brought from home. Yogurt and fruit for breakfast, consumed during our 10:00 AM story meeting; leftovers and/or a homemade salad for lunch, sometimes with especially fragrant homemade Caesar dressing. The food is packed into Tupperware and stacked in a canvas bag from Chicken on the Way, a favourite takeout from my Calgary hometown.

Every morning, arriving at the station by car or by bus, I have my briefcase and lunch bag slung over my shoulder, over my daily uniform: cargo shorts, a logoed hoodie of some kind (usually the New York Yankees) and "thongs" as I know them, "flip-flops" if you prefer (and as my kids insist). For several years my suits and ties have lived in the dressing room at work and the daily TV transformation occurs there.

But on this morning, after seeing the email, I don't pack breakfast or lunch. I do, however, wear shorts and a hoodie. And those thongs.

The email reads terse. But doesn't email always? I don't think it is meant to be. However, the message is clear. I was to meet management off-site at 9:30 AM, in a meeting room at a hotel around the corner.

The signs were all there. And it didn't take a sleuth to connect the dots: a sudden interest in the overnight ratings by a manager who didn't really know a lot about television news; a station-wide staff campaign for ideas on improving newscasts and viewership, with little input sought from the news director and anchor; and most of all, a salary that I knew put a target on my back every second Friday. Perhaps the most telling clue was a surprise visit from the station's former general manager, who had a well-earned reputation for making cuts. He's the same Mr. Fix-It who had lured me to the station nearly a decade earlier.

I check my phone again, reread the email—again, and then check my BC Transit App to see when the #14 departs the University of Victoria bus loop to start its trip across town to Victoria General Hospital. From UVic it's about four or five minutes to my stop. The ride downtown is uneventful, and even though my mind wants to race, I kill the time playing Scrabble on my phone and scanning overnight news on Twitter.

It is shortly before nine when I arrive downtown, and I can't help but notice how utterly ordinary everything seems. At least so far. At least to everyone else. The panhandler at the corner outside the 7-Eleven. The tourists dragging their luggage across the sidewalk at the Carlton Best Western Hotel, where I will return for the off-site meeting at 9:30.

I'm not quite sure what to expect when I get to the station. My access card still opens the door. The lock on my office hasn't been changed. I can log on to my computer. It's now about ten minutes to nine, and suddenly, time is moving very slowly.

What do you do to fill the forty-odd minutes between now and the end? My cluttered office in the far corner of the CTV newsroom is just as I had left it not much more than twelve hours earlier, other than the overnight arrival of the morning papers. A stack of several scripts from the previous night's newscast, marked with a circle around a line of bad copy or some other error—the "circle stack" as it was known, perhaps with derision among some. But the stack isn't filled only with fault; those circled scripts also highlight good writing and storytelling, a clever turn of phrase or good use of pictures and sound. The desk is its usual mess of notes and clippings and to-do lists left undone from the night before. In the corner are two old TVs that beam news at me, unblinking all day, but for now they are still dark. The awards, plaques and pictures covering the wall stare down at me as I sit at my desk, gazing into space, wondering what to do.

What do you do in a situation like this? Fire up the shredder? Start copying contacts and deleting computer files? I do neither. What I do is assume my normal routine, going downstairs to the dressing room to change out of my shorts and hoodie, and put on a suit and tie. Isn't it tradition on Death Row to wear your Sunday best to your execution?

So far there is no outward hint that anything is amiss. This is all pretty normal. Small talk with the security officer in the lobby. A brief discussion with our assignment editor about the coming news of the day. Scanning the papers and websites for stories we already had yesterday, and others we might chase today. Then back to my office to watch the seconds crawl by on the clock on the wall.

I find a welcome distraction when I turn on the TVs. I actually have three in my office, the two in the corner and a nine-inch set on my desk. Always on, usually with the volume up high, competing with the radio and the computer, the phone and someone at the door. No wonder I am easily distracted. (*Wanna ride bikes? Look, there's a squirrel!*) These are old TVs, big obsolete

CRT monitors like you see dumped by renters on the curb with a FREE sign. But they are Sonys and despite the thousands of hours on them since this station, known as "The New VI," had signed on more than a decade earlier, they still have a good picture. Anyway, if there was room in the budget for new flat screens, they should go in the newsroom, not my office, right?

The Sochi Winter Olympics are into their final week. And on the air this morning is the women's gold medal hockey game. Team Canada against the USA. A rematch of the final in Vancouver four years earlier. A chance for a fourth gold medal for the Canadian women. I grab a coffee from the radio station on the third floor. (For some reason, radio coffee is always better than TV coffee.) And I watch the first period.

The distance between the station and the downtown hotel where I have been summoned can be measured in fewer than a hundred steps. But on this mild sunny morning, Victoria's version of late winter, it seems a world away.

Waiting for me, in a small meeting room on the third floor, are the station manager and the regional VP, who flew over from Vancouver to lend support and to represent the corporate hierarchy. Neither one of them is a bad guy. And I still quite like them both, despite what is about to happen next.

As I enter the room, the telltale table is set. One chair on the far side, two on this side, closest to the door. As I have learned over the years, sitting on the firing side, you want a clear path to evacuate the room if things go sideways. On this morning they will not.

"This can't be good," I offer with a smile as I take my place. In a way, I think the two of them, or at least my GM, are more nervous than I am. The manager reads from his script. Always follow the script just in case you have to testify later as to what exactly was said. I almost feel sorry for him having to do this. This is the part they don't put in the management brochure. I too have read a similar message to a teary-eyed employee, often with a lump in my throat.

But on this day, for me, as I listen, there is no lump and there are no tears. And though meetings like this usually take on a surreal, gauzy quality after the word "termination" is uttered, this is all pretty matter-of-fact. No weeping or wailing. No shouting. No angry outburst. Instead we chat for several minutes, discussing in general terms the details of the package, the timeline for an announcement and how to deliver the message.

I agree that it's in everyone's best interest to frame the move positively, if we can. I consider the option of letting on I am resigning, but I have spent my professional life telling the truth and earning peoples' trust. That isn't going to happen.

But in a statement the following Monday, I will announce that we've agreed to part company and that for me the timing is right, leaving the station after nearly a decade. I have in fact chosen to leave (without a fight), but in reality I haven't been presented with much of a list of options from which to choose.

The statement I will offer the *Victoria Times Colonist* talks about my impending fifty-fourth birthday, a milestone for me, reaching the age my dad was when he died. It seems as if the timing is no accident. And truth be told, I'm ready for a change; the fun was starting to go out of it. Better to leave the station this way than feet first.

The statement will be interpreted by many to mean that I've retired, though I never use that word specifically. But if there is face-saving for both sides, my public statement and the station's have taken the high road. Will I have spun the message, and misled the people who invited me into their homes for so many years? I hope not, but I leave that for others to judge.

On this night, I will watch my old newscast to see how they handle the news of my departure. Over the course of two hours I will not be mentioned once, nothing to indicate publicly, as we had agreed, that we've parted on mutual terms. Not that I am looking for a flowery tribute; I expect none. But after ten years as the face of the station, to have been airbrushed into oblivion is, I think, a show of disrespect to our viewers, not to mention to me.

In many ways, what's happening this morning is not coming as a total surprise. I had confided to friends and trusted colleagues that I always knew there was a bullet with my name on it some Friday afternoon. How many times had I said that? But it doesn't happen on Fridays anymore. The HR gurus prefer Tuesday or Thursday mornings so that despondent, suddenly unemployed people don't go home and have the weekend to brood, or worse.

And it's the nature of the business. I saw it happen to my dad in Calgary at CFAC in 1968. My brother got squeezed in Detroit in the 1980s. Broadcasting is like that. And some of my friends in the biz will tell you that you haven't really made it in this industry until you have been blown out, at least once. Fact is, the lifespan of news directors in many markets—especially in the US—is about two years at best. So by that measure I have certainly had a good run. And I will qualify that with "so far."

I came to Victoria in April 1985. I'd had five years working and learning in the BC interior, in Kamloops and Prince George. And I turned a blind eye over the years to many opportunities to leave Vancouver Island. When I had the chance to leave CHEK-TV in 2004 to help steer a floundering news department and station off the rocks, it was irresistible—a chance to reinvent myself without having to leave the island and uproot my family. We had succeeded wildly doing it, and I'd had nearly a decade of having fun while we were at it. I'm lucky. If I have any regrets it is that my departure is happening about a year too soon. I had hoped to continue until at least April 1, 2015, which would have been thirty years to the day after first appearing on the air on the island. Milestones, who needs them?

So now, the meeting in the hotel is over. After about fifteen or twenty minutes—long for meetings like this—there's nothing left to say. I am to take the envelope, read the letter carefully, get some legal advice if I want and get back to management by Monday.

And with that, it is time for handshakes. I suggest that I need to return to the station to grab a few personal belongings—mainly my hoodie, shorts, thongs and briefcase. The task of clearing the clutter in my office and boxing up my on-air wardrobe downstairs can wait. For now, the task at hand is to make a clean exit before the start of our ten o'clock newsroom story meeting. I'll take a couple of days off and we'll figure out what happens by Monday.

So, after an awkward elevator ride, the GM and I walk back to the station. Maybe it isn't that awkward. He's a guy just doing his job, and he's not a bad guy. Meetings such as this are just part of the job description.

I lock up my office after allowing myself a wistful glance over my shoulder. I drop off my keys and phone and security card in the GM's office. Then we shake hands again, this time in the station lobby, in front of the trophy case filled with nearly fifty news and other industry awards we earned on my watch. Leave something better than you found it. I know I did that.

Back on the street, still in a suit, my briefcase and bag of casual clothes slung over my shoulder, I walk off, but this isn't sunset—it's still the morning sun.

They'd offered me a cab ride home. In the old days of staff purges at what was then "The New VI," black Lincoln Town Cars were the harbinger of doom. Town Cars and Ice Cream Cakes. Staff members who had survived previous cuts had a Pavlovian reaction to the first sight of the black sedans, reaching immediately for a banker's box to begin clearing their desks.

I had declined the cab fare, with thanks. I could call Patty or one of my kids to come and get me. Or I could stagger in an aimless fog around the streets of downtown Victoria. Well, that was never really an option. I do neither. Instead I walk straight to the bus stop, the same one where, on any other workday, I would have rushed to after getting off the air at 7:00 PM. And I get on the bus and ride home. No one on the bus but me knows how different things are since my last ride, less than two hours before.

How things have suddenly changed hits me on the way home. Not in the way you might expect. I always kill time on the bus playing Scrabble on my phone. The phone I now no longer have in my hand, as I surrendered it just a few minutes earlier.

That something is up is immediately apparent to our son Hamilton, as I walk in the door, now dressed for work. He was still asleep when I had set out with my secret. Upstairs, Patty is on the phone with a real estate deal. She knows this isn't right. Now come the tears and incredulity, but not from me. I'm sanguine. It's all good.

In the weeks and months since that morning, I realize I have learned an invaluable lesson, however difficult it may have been, or may have seemed at the time. I am here to share that lesson with you and to share some of the stories that have made me who I am.

What follows is not a lurid tell-all, peeling back layer after layer to expose the rot in Canadian broadcast journalism, ripping away the covers to reveal the soft underbelly of local TV news in a medium-sized Canadian city. (Well, maybe we'll have a *bit* of that.) If it's not that, what it is, is my story. And I hope that in sharing my experiences and introducing you to the people in my life, you will know me better. And maybe there is something in my story that will help you in yours. I hope so.

This is the end. But really, it is only the beginning.

# 2
## Clarence

I love the smell of an old radio station. If you've ever had a whiff, you know what I mean. If you haven't smelled one—and there aren't many places left to find one—you might have to use your imagination. These days there are fewer and fewer people who remember what it's like, and fewer and fewer—if any—radio stations that still have that smell.

Old dust cooking on hot vacuum tubes. Threadbare carpet. Stale coffee and cigarette smoke. The vague and almost indiscernible smell of vinyl records. They really do have a scent.

Now, imagine all this in a rabbit warren of tiled corridors and studios separated by thick angled windows and two-way drawers. Walls covered in nicotine-stained acoustical tile. Not the black egg crate foam of today. Those old two-by-two-foot off-white squares pockmarked with holes to deaden the sound. A control room with turntables and open-reel tape machines. A big old ribbon microphone suspended on a spring-loaded arm. A tattered program log covered in cross-out lines and scribbles. On one side, a metal carousel loaded with cartridge tapes—"carts." On the other, a rack in the corner covered with a crisscross tangle of patch cords. Everything feeding into and out of an old console on the counter—probably a McCurdy board—with rows of keys, round dials and a great big vu meter lit up in the middle like a beacon in the dim room.

And then there's the sound. An off-air monitor providing a constant background. If it falls silent it heralds the radio sin of dead air. The back and forth squeaking of a record being cued up on the turntable. The squeal of tape rewinding. Across the hall from the newsroom, the clatter of typewriters and newswires, and the din of ringing telephones.

And the silence. The absolute quiet you feel as much as hear when the heavy studio door closes and the mic turns on, as the soundproof walls and windows close out the rest of the world.

Radio stations don't look or sound or smell like that anymore. Today, a radio station—or a cluster of them—can be run from a laptop computer. Or a couple of servers in a rack in the hallway. But they used to be like that. And those sights and sounds and smells are what will always remind me of Clarence Mack. My father. Some of my earliest childhood recollections are of radio stations. One in particular. CFAC radio in Calgary, where my dad spent most of his broadcasting career during the 1950s and 1960s. This truly was the "Golden Age" of radio, at least for me. My dad was the morning man on the number one radio station in the city. His *Toast and Marmalade* breakfast program was how most Calgarians started their day. CFAC's format in those days was MOR—Middle of The Road—the kind of programming that doesn't really play much anywhere, anymore in radio's modern era. (Later CFAC was big again thanks to a switch to country music, before the eventual and inevitable demise of music-driven AM stations; after rebranding a couple of times, it is now a sports talk station.)

FM radio was then still an obscurity and specific targeting of a demographic or market segment was years away. This was radio for everyone—and families would be together listening to their AM radio in the kitchen every morning, eating breakfast and marching around the table.

My father's radio career began around the end of the Second World War. He served with the Royal Canadian Air Force, but not overseas. He was exempted from overseas duty during the war on account of a broken arm he had suffered as a youth. I think he fell out of a tree. It was not a disability in any way, but it kept him in Canada throughout the war. He was stationed at the Calgary-based RCAF Repair Depot, which helped plant the seed for his lifelong love of aviation, airplanes and airports.

He had come from humble beginnings, born in 1920 in the town of Didsbury, Alberta, about halfway between Calgary and Red Deer. A nondescript farming town first settled by Dutch Mennonites who had come west from Pennsylvania. His parents, about whom I admittedly know little, were of distant Germanic descent via Nebraska.

I don't know much about my grandparents, because all four died either before I was born or when I was very young. I do have some recollection of my dad's parents. His father died at a bus stop on what is now Calgary's Bow Trail, on a Friday night on his way to Stampede Wrestling. He suffered a heart attack and fell face first to the pavement. According to family folklore, doctors say he had died before he hit the ground. That was around 1964.

My dad's mother died a couple of years later. My childhood memories of her consist mostly of my big brother mimicking her—as she would gum her way through Sunday dinner—and of the obligatory drives to and from the nursing home for said meal. One Sunday I remember being especially incensed that I was forced to come for the ride and miss my favourite TV program at the time, *Rat Patrol*—a big deal at age six.

Clarence was tall and thin, with a big mouthful of brilliant white teeth, a feature that my mother always said was part of his appeal. (I'm not sure I inherited his build, but our oldest son

certainly did; Hamilton is lean and lanky like his grandfather.)
My father was enormously talented, with a drive to serve the
community.

He loved airplanes and flying, and that is how he met my
mother. She was a nursing student at the Calgary General Hospital
in the Class of 1941. They were introduced by a mutual friend, and
before long he was taking her on dates to the old airport at McCall
Field for sightseeing flights in biplanes over Calgary. They married
shortly after she graduated from nursing school, and he travelled
to Toronto to enroll in Lorne Greene's prestigious Academy of
Radio Arts. Long before he was known as *Bonanza* patriarch Ben
Cartwright, Canadian-born CBC alum Greene founded a hothouse
to grow Canadian talent for the burgeoning radio industry. The
list of alumni reads like a who's who of the radio stars of the day,
including many who went on to success in show business in the
US. One of them was a classmate of Clarence's, Leslie Nielsen.
Either he owed my dad ten bucks or it was the other way around,
but that story always got dusted off when we would see Nielsen on
television or in movies.

My mother had stayed in Calgary to take care of her ailing
parents and, as is often the case in life as viewed in retrospect, that
had a major impact on Clarence's career and our lives. The CBC
was vacuuming up the students of the Lorne Greene Academy as
soon as they graduated, and my dad was offered a job with the
CBC in Montreal. In what must have been a difficult choice, he
declined and returned to Calgary so that my mom could continue
to care for her parents. If he was ever bitter about that, I don't
know if he let on. But it might have had something to do with his
mild disdain for the CBC.

His first job in Calgary radio was at CJCJ, which later became
the Top 40 station I listened to as a kid, CKXL. Leslie Nielsen also
put in a stint at CJCJ, which may be where the ten bucks came in.
After a couple of years there, Clarence moved to CFAC, which he
helped turn into the dominant radio station in the city. The station

was founded by the *Calgary Herald* newspaper in 1922, and in the early days its studios were in the old Greyhound bus building. The only reason I recall that is because we used to have a huge Boston fern houseplant, and I was always reminded that it used to reside in the lobby of the Greyhound building studios. Weird, the stuff you remember.

CFAC was owned at the time by a company called Taylor, Pearson and Carson, which went on to become Selkirk, one of the big players in Canadian broadcasting at the time. It in turn was swallowed up by Maclean-Hunter, which was then eaten by Rogers. The station is now part of the Rogers radio cluster in Calgary, sharing downtown studio space with the Rogers TV properties, City and Omni.

Clarence wore many hats over the years, including the emblematic white Smithbilt cowboy hat during his time on the Calgary Stampede board of directors, one of many such posts. He was the director of CFAC's drama department, hosted the top-rated morning program *Toast and Marmalade* and went on to become Program Director. He helped launch the careers of aspiring broadcasters, people like Betty Kennedy, who went on to greater fame at Toronto's CFRB and on CBC's *Front Page Challenge*. He had put her on the panel of *State Your Case*, one of the earliest radio talk shows of its kind, and until then a male bastion.

I have fond childhood memories of the CFAC studios on Seventeenth Avenue in Calgary. Especially that old radio station smell. There was a large studio where the radio plays were performed and recorded, under my father's direction as Drama Director. His love of acting would also extend to the Calgary stage. From Workshop 14 to the boards of the Jubilee Auditorium, Clarence distinguished himself as an actor, best remembered for such roles as the Stage Manager in *Our Town* and Clarence Darrow in *Inherit the Wind*. One of my great regrets is losing my collection of radio plays he produced and performed in. I had a box full of old seven-inch open-reel audiotapes, irreplaceable copies of radio dramas, with titles like *The Devil's Instrument* and *We All Hate Toronto* (even then, that was a popular theme in Calgary). I had the tapes stored with all of my belongings in the garage of a rental suite in Calgary in 1980, and all of the stuff was taken away and dumped as garbage. The rest of it I wasn't overly worried about. Losing the box of tapes still bugs me. I'll never forgive the guy who was my roommate at the time.

I have three scrapbooks of my dad's. They're full of pictures, newspaper clippings and memorabilia from his career. Much of it has to do with his community service. He was active with many organizations, not the least of which, ironically, was the Canadian Cancer Society. He served as an alderman for seven terms from 1955 to 1963, and he ran for mayor twice, losing the election both times. I wasn't born yet for the first run and was really too young to remember much about the second, but I have vague and hazy recollections of the campaign and his disappointment on election night. I think the rejection got to him. In one of the scrapbooks, there is a clipping from the *Calgary Herald* that shows a photo of him listening to our old stereo console as the votes were being counted and the result was becoming apparent. He looks sad and that always made me sad too.

I was fourteen when he died from cancer, so all of my memories of him were forged in those impressionable childhood and early teen years. He was a different dad, I think, to my sister, Leilani, and me than he was to my brothers, Gary and Darrel. Darrel was killed in an accidental shooting before I was born.

Darrel was an unusual child. He may have been a genius. Today, he surely would have undergone psychological testing to see if there was anything wrong. He had a high IQ but was quiet and withdrawn. There was an incident one day, when he was five or six years old, in which he disappeared from their old apartment. My parents were frantically looking for him, and after a search had been mobilized, he came home, nonchalant, after riding the transit bus all day. My mom said he told her that he had seen them all looking for him as the bus drove by the apartment each time.

He had wanted a gun and my dad got him a rifle. My dad took him to the local rod and gun club for training in gun safety. The rifle was disassembled and locked up in separate locations. The bullets were locked up elsewhere. But one day, when Darrel was twelve, somehow he was able to get the keys and get the gun. He was in the garage of our old house on Thirty-Second Avenue. It was New Year's Eve day, 1956. My dad picked up my mom from her job at the Associate Clinic downtown where she was a nurse. My brother Gary got a ride home with them. He had taken the bus downtown to buy a record at the Hudson's Bay store. He was excited to come home and play his new 45, the number one song that week, "Green Door." I always used to think it was by Elvis Presley, but the hit recording of the day was by Jim Lowe. It didn't matter who it was. This was a song that would never be played in our home again.

When they arrived, Darrel was in the garage, dying. He had somehow shot himself, and it was my brother who found him. He died in the hospital hours later. Was it an accident? Only he knew. But I know that my father blamed himself, and the guilt he felt ate away at him, and probably contributed to his own death years later. I don't think any of them, especially my brother Gary, who was eight at the time, benefited from much in the way of grief counselling or post-traumatic support. This was the late 1950s and people didn't do that. I know Gary suffered as a result, and what he saw that day would haunt him, one of the demons he fought all his life. My dad never talked about it and it wasn't until years later that my mom told us in detail what had happened.

I think he was a mellower dad with my sister and me—older and, sadly, wiser. My sister Leilani was born less than a year and a half after Darrel died, and me, by accident, about another eighteen months later. I'm surprised they didn't move after the shooting happened. I'm not sure I could have ever set foot in that garage again, if I had witnessed it.

Calgary in the early 1960s was on the cusp of the oil boom. And many of the things that have helped it grow and prosper over the years got their start while Clarence was on city council. He was part of the early planning that created the city's system of "trails," freeways that made it possible to get from one corner of the city to the other in less than twenty minutes. At least, it used to be that way. And he was a proponent of preservation, helping lead the campaign to keep Nose Hill as a green space.

He wasn't much for self-aggrandizement. The city wanted to honour his contributions by naming a street after him but he declined. He also wouldn't allow his name to go on a plaque to recognize his work to save an old steam locomotive from the scrapyard in the 1950s. It sits today at the entrance to Heritage Park, but for years was on display at the Tourism Centre on Ninth Avenue. A columnist for the *Herald*, Ken Liddell, had written about the loss of the big old CPR steam locomotives, the 5900 series, which were being replaced by diesels. Clarence created a club to raise money to buy one. He encouraged his listeners to join the 5900 Club. For a dollar, they received a membership card, and that was it. But enough people got onboard and he raised enough money, one dollar at a time, to preserve this piece of Canadian history. Months before he died, we returned to Calgary in July 1974, to attend a ceremony to thank him and mark the twentieth anniversary of the preservation.

He stayed at CFAC until 1968. And the end of his twenty-two-year career at the station played out the way it usually does—little did I realize, until my own experience decades later. He had been promoted to Program Director at the station and was no longer on the air with the morning show every day. There was more competition for listeners, and the station's dominance had slipped. The British Invasion of the early- to mid-1960s had fuelled the popularity of rock and roll. And though he argued against it, CFAC had changed its format to challenge CKXL. It didn't work. Ratings fell and he was left holding the bag. The GM of the day blamed him, though he had tried to stop the change. So in April 1968, just days after the assassination of Dr. Martin Luther King, Clarence Mack was given an ultimatum: relinquish the duties of Program Director and go back onto the morning show, or go clean out your office. He was gone by the end of the day. He was a week shy of his forty-eighth birthday.

After leaving CFAC, my father got out of radio for a while. He'd had a long association with the Calgary Flying Club. He had his pilot's licence and rented small planes from the club, mostly Piper Cubs and Chipmunks. The club had an arrangement with CFAC on a leased aircraft for daily traffic reports. I think this was partly my dad's way of flying every day, but it was also a reflection of him as a broadcast innovator. Airborne traffic reporting was not common yet in Canadian radio.

So, if not radio as a career, then something to do with flying. And that's how he became the General Manager of the Calgary Flying Club. I suppose the many trips to the airport as a nine- and ten-year-old kid have something to do with my lifelong fascination with airports and planes (though I never did get my pilot's licence, even though Patty bought me an introductory lesson for a birthday present). I have vivid recollections of the old flying club hangar, with offices, a coffee shop, and a small flight simulator I loved to sit in. It's long gone now, of course. Around this time, with the 1970s around the corner, the phenomenal growth of Calgary demanded a bigger airport. The old McCall Field buildings were bulldozed for a new terminal to the north, and the flying club would move west, out of town to the new Springbank airport, now barely beyond the city limits.

The flying club gig was okay for a while, but eventually the internal politics of the board of directors, and a longing for the airwaves, grounded my dad's change of career at the airport. He was off the air and a fish out of water. Clarence Mack was soon back on the radio in Calgary at CHQR, before it became a news/talk station, still playing "beautiful music." But it was a long way from *Toast and Marmalade*. Maybe he was spurred on to change by the dawn of the new decade. The year 1970 was a turning point. He had begun to sour on Calgary. The people he had helped through his years of local community and political service were suddenly nowhere to be found when he needed a break.

He was an amazing radio talent. He had a beautiful voice, recordings of which I have precious few. And he was a brilliant producer and a natural programmer. He knew how to connect with his listeners, and there was a new radio audience waiting that had never heard anyone quite like him.

# 3
# Salmon Arm

Toward the end of our time in Calgary, it was clear that the Stampede City had lost its lustre—at least for my dad, who had given so much to it. But the notion of moving away was a bolt out of the blue.

In early 1971, Clarence put an ad in the *Broadcaster* magazine, which was then the industry bible in Canada. I wish I had a copy of it today. A little ad: "Seasoned broadcast veteran looking for new challenge and opportunity. Willing to relocate." Just one column inch that would change our lives. The blind-box ad in *Broadcaster* was answered by Bob Hall, who co-owned a radio station in the small town of Salmon Arm, BC.

If you drive from Calgary to Vancouver, it is almost exactly the halfway point.

Clarence fell in love with the place. And he thrived being back on the air. There is something magical about small-town radio and the place it occupies in people's lives. He brought a level of professionalism and a big market sound that the station had never enjoyed. And he swallowed his pride to do it. But he was having fun on the radio again. Soon his morning show was a ratings leader in larger nearby markets, Vernon and Kamloops.

Named for the section of Shuswap Lake around which it is built, Salmon Arm is the main trading centre for the region. The CP Rail mainline snakes around the lakeshore and passes through the middle of town; not far away, an endless stream of transport trucks rumble along the Trans-Canada Highway bisecting the community. In the summer, there is a thriving tourist industry, but in the winter it gets pretty quiet. The hospital and school district were the region's biggest employers at the time, and the forest industry is still a major player, though there are fewer mills these days. But there was and is a service industry, a small downtown area and lots of orchards, mostly apple and cherry.

I must admit that, as a kid, all I knew about it was the town's funny name, which I'd seen on the highway signs when, like most Calgarians heading to the Okanagan, we turned south at Sicamous to the east. We may not have known much about it, but Salmon Arm grew on us quickly. At least, it grew on my dad in a hurry.

There wasn't a lot to do in those days, other than go to Shuswap Lake. Not a lot of amenities then. We would drive thirty-five miles each way to Vernon to swim in the public pool. Salmon Arm was a picturesque resort town that didn't seem to know what kind of a goldmine it was sitting on. We marvelled at what seemed to us to be backward small-town thinking. No appetite for resort development along the shore, more concern for bird nesting areas. I get it now.

Clarence moved to Salmon Arm first, ahead of the rest of the family, in the spring of 1971, and lived at a boarding house called "Gabe's Bunkhouse." The couple who ran it, Gabe and Vi Pfoh, were local legends. She was "mom" to everyone in town, especially the young men who lived there, many of them rookie RCMP officers on their first posting. She was one of the hardest-working people I have ever known, suffering from a condition that wouldn't let her sleep more than a couple of hours a day. The rest of the time she worked.

Clarence's new radio station, CKXR, was known as "The Big R, First Voice West of the Rockies." That claim to fame was a legitimate one, because the Salmon Arm signal was rebroadcast from repeater transmitters seventy miles to the east in Revelstoke, and farther still at the other end of the Rogers Pass, in Golden. For the thousands of Albertans and others on the highway heading west for their BC vacation, the first signal their car radio would pick up was "The Big R."

The station was co-owned by Bob Hall, in partnership with Walter Gray, who would later, in the 1990s, become a longtime mayor of Kelowna. Eventually the partnership split, with Gray taking over the company's Kelowna station, CKIQ. Bob Hall would take CKXR. Later he would make millions bringing cable television to the Shuswap area (there was none when we lived there). My first recollection of hearing my voice on the radio came via CKIQ, where my dad and I recorded a commercial one summer. I was the child's voice in a father-and-son spot, a public service announcement about forest fires and campfire safety. It won an award.

Hall was a decent man, though I think in a way he might have been jealous of my dad. Clarence took the job, went back onto mornings and soon this little station was winning the breakfast ratings over stations in neighbouring cities and towns. Bob realized, I think, that he had hired a guy with infinitely more talent and experience in the business, but from what I could tell as a kid, he was generally fair with my dad. And years later he would show his kindness to me.

It must have stuck in Clarence's craw, though, to have things come to this. Years on city council in Calgary, twice a candidate for mayor, truly the toast of the town, now working at a tiny small-town radio station and living in a double-wide trailer, which is a story in itself.

We had made a number of trips from Calgary to look for houses but nothing grabbed us. The one place we liked had a beautiful lake view, but we didn't know the local geography yet and it seemed like it was in the middle of nowhere. It wasn't. But the real reason we didn't make an offer was that my mom's spidey senses were tingling; something about the place didn't feel right. A mother's intuition.

One day, and I recall it vividly, I was with my parents, grocery shopping at the Woodward's Food Floor in Calgary's Chinook Mall. (Don't you miss Woodward's?) My parents bumped into an old radio colleague. They were telling him about moving to Salmon Arm and the fruitless house hunt. And his reply was, "I'd live in a goddamn trailer if I had a chance to move to Salmon Arm!"

So, that's what we did.

There was a guy named Brian Sidorsky who had a furniture store in Calgary and also sold mobile homes on the McLeod Trail. He was known for his goofy TV commercials. Every town has a salesman who smashes TVs with a sledgehammer on television, and he was ours. We checked out his show lot and found a nice double-wide "modular home" (this sounds nicer than "trailer"). The hitch and wheels did come off and it was about the size of a modest regular house. But it was still a trailer. Let's be honest. If Clarence felt he was going down a rung on the social ladder, he didn't say. I didn't care. I was an eleven-year-old boy moving to a town on a lake, and the money we saved by not buying a house meant we could buy a boat instead. We actually bought two. The first one was stolen before we took possession of it. Thankfully my dad had already purchased insurance. That was typical of him. The boat was last seen passing through Revelstoke, being towed eastbound over the Rogers Pass, full of stolen water skis and outboard motors.

I didn't have a problem being a Trailer Park Boy (though it would be years before we'd find out what *that* meant). Our spot was at the entrance, so there was no having to drive past over-turned Pontiacs or fridges on the porch. The park was in an old apple orchard and overlooked a strawberry farm. I picked berries for a couple of seasons. Backbreaking work and it turned me off strawberries for years. My mother, I learned later, felt the stigma of living in a trailer—oops, I mean mobile home. It may have bugged my mom, but she didn't make an issue of it at the time. And I know it kind of bugged my sister. Actually, there wasn't much about Salmon Arm that didn't bug Leilani. At least at first. She was thirteen when we moved from Calgary and that's a harder age to face a move than it was for me at age eleven. She couldn't understand how I wasn't mad that I now faced one more year of elementary school in Salmon Arm. Had we stayed in Calgary, I would be going into junior high school for Grade 7.

But I didn't care. I was unfazed by the notion of picking up and leaving Calgary. My sister was not, and in fairness, it was a more difficult transition for her, I suppose. She was in junior high already, connecting with a new network of friends, and had made the girls' basketball team. She was not keen, to say the least.

My mom, who had spent her entire life in Calgary, growing up in the house where she was born, had some trepidation I am sure. But she kept it to herself in support of my dad.

For me it was high adventure. I didn't care about Grade 7. I quite liked our elementary school, which was close by. My friends and I liked it so much that we went there during the summer. Someone had discovered that if you kicked the doors of the gymnasium fire escape in just the right place, they'd pop wide open, and there was no alarm. I was never the kind of kid who would have gotten into anything like this, but peer pressure being what it is, I was lured along one afternoon. Our intent was without malice. All we wanted to do, and all I ever participated in, was illicit floor hockey in the gym. And it got to be habit forming. We'd kick open the door and turn on the lights, grab the gear and play hockey in the gym for hours. We never took a thing and never really explored the empty school beyond the gym.

Unfortunately, as more players joined the game, word spread

of the side-door entrance at South Broadview Elementary. Some guys who were not part of our group broke in late one night and ransacked the place, pouring paint and glue down the length of the long corridor running from one end of the single-storey school to the other, then setting it on fire. It burned to the ground.

As I recall, the RCMP made at least one arrest in the arson. I don't remember who it was, a local punk who I think went to jail for it. We were mad about the vandalism and the fire. We were also worried that we might be implicated, and ticked off that our underground summertime activity centre was destroyed. Our role in those extracurricular activities never came to light—until now. I trust the statute of limitations has run out.

The passage of time is an interesting thing. When you are young and living in the moment, everything seems so important and what turns out to have been a brief time seemed to have stretched out forever. That's kind of how it was for me in Salmon Arm. I only lived there for seven years, but we packed a lot in, and the memories of that time are still vivid, even if some are hazy. It was the '70s after all.

Until I took the bullet at CTV, I used to always be able to say, with some self-aggrandizement, that I had been continuously employed since the age of eleven. And it's true. My first job was at Gabe's Bunkhouse, where my dad had first stayed in Salmon Arm. I worked weekends doing odd jobs at the boarding house, mostly changing beds and cleaning. Later I would work in their catering businesses, which meant that for several years, I attended most of the wedding receptions in town.

After that I worked through high school at the local Kentucky Fried Chicken, one of the few name brand fast-food franchises in town (the first McDonald's wouldn't open until years later). And I helped my dad at the radio station on weekends after he got sick. I learned how to program the big IGM automation machine, threading the big open-reel tapes, loading audio cartridges into the carousels and setting the clock to trigger the machine commands. Many radio stations today are automated with voice tracking for most of the day, but in the early 1970s this was still cutting edge. American evangelist Garner Ted Armstrong was able to deliver the Good Word to the Shuswap on his *The World Tomorrow* program, thanks to me.

The KFC years were a good earner for me through high school, though I was never any good with money and managed to save little. Surprisingly, I never got sick of KFC and still consider it a treat. The job also gave my friends a place to hang out on a Friday night. There might have been no customers, but the parking lot was full and the kitchen packed with my friends, partying out of sight under the big exhaust fans and eating as much fried chicken as they could choke down. I was also popular at parties after work, having somehow cooked buckets more chicken than could be sold that night, so what could I do but take some with me?

The KFC was also the scene of an incident that may have saved my life. After my dad died in 1974, my mom sold me their Mustang. It was a red convertible that my parents had bought new in Calgary in 1966. I still recall the shock and awe as a six-year-old kid, that my parents were buying a Mustang convertible. I would spend hours behind the wheel in our Calgary garage, and at the curb on Thirty-Second Avenue, pretending to race it. When I turned sixteen, my mom sold it to me for the princely sum of five hundred dollars. I was over the moon. Then, one week to the day after getting my driver's licence, I smashed it up in the KFC parking lot.

It was a Friday afternoon, and it was payday. I pulled in after school to pick up my cheque, along with a chicken breast and a rib, and was on my way out the back door. In those days KFC franchises in BC were known as "Ernie's Take Home" and were owned by the White Spot chain of restaurants. The raw chicken would be trucked in from Vancouver, bagged, in big silver bins packed with ice. There would always be loose chicken fat in the bags of cut-up pieces, and one of our favourite kitchen games was throwing the fat at each other. The blobs were ice-cold. They flew like a fastball and when they hit, they'd splatter and stick. And they'd sting. It was great fun.

As I was leaving that afternoon with chicken and cheque, I grabbed a big blob of fat and threw it as hard as I could at my co-worker Detlef Doose. He was one of the early adapters of car stereos, with a top-of-the-line Craig Powerplay eight-track player that was worth more than the old Mazda he drove. Detlef would run speaker wire from his trunk into the back door of the kitchen and blast his music while he worked.

My fat bomb found its mark, splatting on the side of his head. I knew there would be retaliation, so I ran out the back of the restaurant, past his car and blaring speakers. I think he was playing Supertramp at the time. He usually was.

The roof on the Mustang was down and I jumped over the driver's door like Adam West getting into the Batmobile. I gunned it and popped the clutch, turning my head back to see where he was, ready to duck the flying fat. When I looked around, I was a second away from slamming into the side of a parked GMC Jimmy, in which sat a woman from Sicamous eating a bucket of popcorn. It went flying. She was knocked sideways. And the front end of the Mustang crumpled as irresistible force met immovable object.

Blood gushed from my nose, which had hit the steering wheel. I'm lucky I wasn't launched over the windshield, since I hadn't had time to do up my seatbelt in the heat of the Fat Fight. I was okay. She was okay. Their Jimmy was okay. The Mustang was not. The hood looked like an accordion. Steam was rising from the wreck as the radiator fluid pooled around our feet.

Back into the KFC I went, through the kitchen and into the customer waiting area to announce to the woman's husband that I had just driven into their parked truck. They were kind, and so was the rookie RCMP officer who rolled up a couple of minutes later. He could have loaded up my new driver's licence with demerit points and slapped me with a big fine. But he took mercy on me, explaining how I should take this opportunity to learn a lesson.

And I did. After that I was the most careful sixteen-year-old on the road. And I'm sure that it saved me. Small towns have a sad habit of losing young people in car accidents, especially in the summer. And when I walk through the Mount Ida Cemetery to visit my dad, I can also find the names of many friends and classmates whose promise was cut short on the highway. I got lucky.

I got the Mustang fixed and have driven it the rest of my life. After moving to Victoria in the mid-eighties, I restored it to undo the ravages of daily driving in Prince George. I still have it today but even in Victoria only drive it in the summer. My own kids are now casting a covetous eye on it. They're going to have to wait, although they're already more sensible now than I was at their age.

If I could do anything differently as a kid growing up in Salmon Arm, it would be to have applied myself more in school. I was always a good student but was a bit of a smartass in class and took the path of least resistance.

I had skipped Grade 1 in Calgary. Skipped is probably the wrong word. Advanced is what they called it then. After a few weeks in the classroom at King Edward (one of Calgary's many sandstone schools built in the early 1900s, with a separate entrance for boys and girls, now converted to condos), my parents were called in to approve my move to Grade 2. It was mainly because of my ability to read already, especially to read aloud. Maybe that was an omen.

So I was always in a group of kids a year older than me, which might explain why I never made the varsity sports teams. I think the best I ever did was the B squad in high school basketball, and I was big enough to make the rugby team in high school (there was unfortunately no football), but I quit after my first game, or maybe it was just an especially rough practice. I didn't want cauli-flower ears and thought I had broken my nose already. Hockey was out of the question because I was born with flat feet. If you follow my footsteps on the beach, you'll think you're walking behind Fred Flintstone. The fallen or never-existent arches put me in agony after a few minutes in skates. A couple of laps around the rink and I'm done. There was also the issue of my teeth. My mom was obsessed with us not breaking our teeth, so hockey was a non-starter, at least on ice.

The age gap may have made more of a difference when I was younger. By high school it didn't matter. But by then I had engrained some pretty poor study habits and was always content to just get by. I started Grade 10 in the fall of 1974, the year my dad died. I didn't realize it at the time, but understandably, that had knocked me sideways.

By the time I was in Grade 12, I was really mailing it in. We were more interested in having fun, which meant a lot of driving around the small town, partying in the woods and on the lake and disappearing down logging roads. I am so glad our kids are much more sensible about drinking and driving.

The nadir of my high school academic career came in my senior year when I bombed out of English 12. It is a stain I wear today. Imagine failing English. I actually didn't fail it but had skipped so many classes that several weeks into the fall, my English teacher told me to quit coming because I could do no better than an "Incomplete" for my final grade. Frankly, it suited me fine. She was a nice enough woman but was a bit too much of a hippie for my taste, gliding into class in gauzy flowing blouses, peasant skirts and paisley leotards. She would put the desks in a circle and launch into some mystical mumbo-jumbo that turned me off. In retrospect, it sounds like I should have taken advantage of it. My teachers were cutting me some slack given my personal circumstances.

Unfortunately, it was too late in the year to transfer into

another English class, so I wouldn't have the required credits to graduate that summer. This was unthinkable but unavoidable. In an act of kindness, the school included me in our graduating class, the Class of 1977, on the proviso that I return for one more semester that fall, to make up English and one other credit.

What happened then gave me an early appreciation for the need to teach students in their own style, recognizing their individual strengths and needs. I was now in an old-school English class taught by one of the eldest teachers in the school, a woman I liked a lot who taught the traditional way: creative writing assignments, literature, fundamentals of grammar. I aced the course. I only had one other class, so it was an easy term to make up everything I needed for my high school diploma. Plus, in the end, I was in the age group I should have been all along. Glynne Green, aka Grider, one of my best friends from the time, who still is today, was in that bunch.

It's funny how high school is the real world in microcosm. What we learn goes far beyond the curriculum in the classroom. Maybe that's why those lessons and experiences are seared into our memory for a lifetime. I liked school. Maybe I would have liked it even more if I had tried just a little bit harder, but maybe not.

Would I be any further ahead in life had I applied myself? Probably not. It might have changed the course of my life. I already knew I wanted to get into broadcasting, and with my mother's support and intervention (seeking advice from no lesser a journalistic luminary as Charles Lynch), I was accepted into the Southern Alberta Institute of Technology (SAIT) broadcast program that fall. If I had been a better student, maybe I would have gone to university instead. Except I didn't know then, any better than I know now, what else I would have spent my life doing other than this.

I'm sure I could have applied myself a little more thoroughly at SAIT too. But I got a great education that has served me well. The SAIT broadcast journalism program is among the best in Canada, with alumni running newsrooms and stations across the country.

While attending SAIT I was living with two buddies from Salmon Arm, Dave Somers and Ken Kendall. Dave was getting his start in the funeral business, Ken bounced from one odd job to another and I worked part-time after school. I loved my job as a bellman at the CP Hotel at the Calgary airport. Until CTV it was the only time I've ever been fired.

Looking back on the Salmon Arm years that were cut too short for Clarence, I can't help but wonder where it all might have led. There was interest in him from CKNW, the powerhouse "top dog" on BC's Lower Mainland, which was in its prime. He was approached by the Progressive Conservatives to seek the nomination for the 1974 federal election. He would certainly have won and I suspect we wouldn't have been in Salmon Arm for long.

But it didn't happen. In late 1973 he developed a nagging cough, and I think he knew something wasn't right. An X-ray revealed a shadow on one of his lungs. The diagnosis was cancer. Like many people of his time, he had smoked, but not heavily. And he had quit immediately when the US Surgeon General's 1961 report drew the link between smoking and lung cancer. He had a pipe for a few years, but it was usually unlit.

Because we were still recent transplants to Salmon Arm, my parents decided he should have the surgery in Calgary, at Foothills Hospital, where my sister would also be treated for lung cancer thirty-five years later. He had the surgery, a large incision on his side under his arm, mid-ribcage, like a smiley face from front to back. Doctors removed the lower half of his left lung.

After the surgery he stayed with our old Calgary neighbours, the Letendres, while he underwent radiation treatment. He would have chemotherapy at home in Salmon Arm. Today's effective anti-nauseant drugs didn't exist then, and the chemo made him very sick. I used to give him backrubs to try to make him feel better. He also developed a case of shingles, which was extremely painful.

I don't know if I let myself realize at the time that he was going to die. I don't think I did. And as I write this, I am now at the age he was when he died, fifty-four. I knew he was young, but when you're a kid you don't really have an appreciation of your parents' age; they're old, they're your parents.

He did return to work after the surgery and I used to go into the radio station with him. There was a long flight of stairs at the entrance, and I'd help him and carry the portable oxygen tank he needed to help him breathe. But even with that, he sounded great. He had such a beautiful voice and delivery. The kind of old-school radio talent you don't seem to come across anymore.

As my father's health deteriorated, he was in and out of the hospital, Shuswap Lake General. My mom was nursing there, having returned to work months earlier when he got sick. She went to work at 7:00 AM on the morning of November 28, 1974. He'd been admitted a couple of days earlier, but there was no indication that the end was near. It was not palliative care at that point. When my mom got to the hospital, she went straight to see him, to say good morning before going to her ward for the day. The door to his room was closed; the nursing supervisor and his doctor were waiting. She knew.

He had died peacefully during the night. Nurses will tell you that people usually die around 3:00 AM. He had spent much of the evening chatting with one of his nurses, who was a friend of my mother's. In his room were a few things we had brought from home, including a painting done by a family friend, Bette Russell, in the style of southern Alberta landscape artist Roland Gissing. It was a scene from the foothills west of Calgary, wheat stooks in a field, with the Rockies in the distance. At one point, in a painkiller-induced haze, my dad thought the stooks were sheepdogs. I've never been able to look at the painting the same way since.

A friend drove my mom home. It was snowing, and my sister and I were getting ready for school. When she came in the door, we knew, before she said a word. I remember we sat together in the living room for a long time, crying. We would pull together and get through this. I promised I would take care of them, now the man of the house at fourteen.

The rest of the next few weeks is a blur. There is a sense of being in limbo between a death and the funeral, something I have experienced all too many times since. But this was the first time. My brother arrived from Windsor, and I think he felt compelled to take the lead. But we had things under control. There may have been a couple of tense moments during the arrangements, but everyone was just trying to do their best. I will always remember an act of kindness by the station owner, Bob Hall, who draped his leather coat over me while I stood shivering in the falling snow at my dad's graveside burial service.

I try not to go through life with too many regrets. But one of them is a choice I made the night before he died. The hospital in Salmon Arm is about a block away from the high school. I was at the school rehearsing for a play that evening, and I was going to visit him afterwards. I decided not to, and I would never get the chance again. If I could change that, I would. But how can you know?

In the haze of the days after my dad died, one particular event stands out. Our dog, Kee-Kee, was hit by a car and killed. He was the family dog but was always my dad's pet. He was cool, a Keeshond, which was a good-looking breed of Dutch barge dog, with a big black and grey mane that made him look a little bit like a lion. He had gotten grumpy in old age and would growl and snarl when you told him he was sweet. We thought this was great sport. He'd bare his teeth but never bite.

Kee-Kee was street smart and would go off for hours at a time but always come home. So when he was out one night, we thought nothing of it. Until the high school gym teacher, who lived a mile or so away, came to our door to tell us our dog was dead. He'd been hit by a car outside their home. I don't know if dogs have the capacity to be suicidal, but, somehow, I have trouble believing Kee-Kee's death was an accident.

None of us knows how much time we have. Losing my dad at an early age taught me a lot of things, and it made me something of a fatalist. I've learned to make sure the people you love know it. And I've learned that we have to accept the things we cannot change.

I thought it was terribly unfair that my dad was taken from us so soon. But I somehow did not lose faith in God. I am more spiritual than religious, but I did not turn away from faith. I think my sister did. We had never been a big churchgoing family. Our parents put us kids in Sunday school in Calgary and we were in the church choir, but they stopped making us go when I kept fainting during the service. It wasn't because of a medical condition or anything, just a long-winded minister and a choir loft that heated up like a chimney. I also don't know why we had to stand for the whole thing. But on several occasions my parents would look up just as I was keeling over or getting carried out. So they said we could stop if we wanted.

My dad's headstone in Mount Ida Cemetery reads, "Had his life been longer, his candle might not have shone as brightly." It's a quote my mom found, originally in reference to Janis Joplin. He would not have liked her nor approved of her music or lifestyle. But the quote really captured him and his life. He burned bright even if his flame went out way too soon.

As I write this, it is forty years to the day since my dad died. And it is most appropriate that, as I write this, I am listening to the sound of the surf pounding the shore in Mexico. My dad loved Mexico, though I think not as much as Hawaii. He was nuts about Hawaii. My parents bought an acre on the Big Island in the early 1960s. It's pretty much all lava, but I still have it. He never got to see it. The closest he came to his Little Grass Shack was our rumpus room in Calgary, a Polynesian paradise to rival Trader Vic's.

My parents were among the first people I know of to travel regularly to Hawaii and Mexico. They went to Acapulco in the 1950s, when it was the playground of Hollywood's rich and famous, the domain of the likes of Frank Sinatra. They travelled to Hawaii before it became a state. And my dad insisted on bringing us kids on almost every trip. That's a habit I inherited, and our kids have him to thank.

I wonder sometimes if he was not unlike the George Bailey character in *It's a Wonderful Life*, a man with an insatiable craving to see the world, who never got everywhere he'd hoped.

# 4

# Patty Love

**D**o you believe in love at first sight? I do. At least, I do now. I know there was a spark when I first laid eyes on Pat Moores walking toward me in a hallway at CHEK TV in April 1985. I'd been at the station only a week or so and had already heard a lot about her from other staff. She had been away in Parksville, taping on-location shoots for the *Ida Clarkson Show*, a popular local daytime talk show. I had already seen her name on a cosmetology certificate hanging in the makeup room at the station. She was certified as a makeup artist, but that wasn't her job. She was a production assistant, working in the newsroom and on other shows. There was something that hit me when I saw her name, and later saw her. She says she had a similar feeling when she saw the station bulletin board and the announcement of my hiring.

For some reason the notice identified me including my middle name, Hudson Hamilton Mack. "Oh, the third?" she asked sarcastically.

She says she also felt something the night she and the rest of the Ida Clarkson crew were gathered around their television in the Parksville hotel room, watching the late news on CHEK. I was making my Victoria debut, and the fact of the matter was, I felt like crap that night. I had come down with the flu days before leaving Prince George for Victoria, and a stop at my mom's in Salmon Arm en route hadn't helped me shake the bug. But I wasn't going to call in sick on my first day.

Then, a week later, Pat (as she called herself then) and I were finally bumping into each other and introducing ourselves.

"Oh, you're the makeup lady," I blurted out, thinking immediately what a stupid thing that was to say. She didn't notice. We hit it off immediately. And one of the things that attracted me to her, and vice versa, which is still a big part of our happy marriage, was her sense of humour. She made me laugh, and she still does.

We worked together on the late news at CHEK. I looked forward to seeing her at work every afternoon, but she was seeing somebody else and had been for some time. He also worked at the station, which made things a little complicated.

One night we were out with a group of people after the news, and we all went to a co-worker's apartment after having a drink downtown. Another member of the crew, who had the hots for Pat, was about to jump into her car for a ride before I intervened. He never liked me after that (and years later was awkwardly one of the employees I inherited when I joined The New VI). It was the weekend of Victoria's Swiftsure Yacht Race, which has always been an unofficial anniversary of sorts for us.

I was living at the time in a tiny apartment suite on the top floor (more like the attic) of an old heritage house in Victoria's Cook Street Village. Pat was sharing a house with her best friend Debby Derry, with whom she's been pals since elementary school.

Pat and I would talk for hours on the phone, though at times I would have to use the payphone outside the grocery store on the corner. (Bad credit and lousy money management had followed me from Prince George. I soon got my act together.)

Patty (which is what I call her now) wasn't always on the night shift, and when she wasn't, I would find out where to locate her after the late news. If it was a Thursday or Friday night, it was usually with her girlfriends at The Sting, a now-disappeared disco in the bowels of Victoria's Strathcona Hotel. I always thought the place was pretty greasy, but she and her friends liked it. The problem was I would show up after midnight and they'd had a head start.

At some point Debby warned Pat that she would have to deal with her boyfriend and decide if she wanted to break up and get out of a dead-end relationship, since she seemed to have made a connection with me. Eventually, that's what happened, and he was out of the picture, though not really completely out, since we still saw him at work. We tried to be discreet at the station, at least at first. Although there was no shortage of couples on staff at CHEK at the time, and most people knew we were one of them.

The house Pat and Debby shared got sold and they moved out on their own. Patty and I found her a great upstairs suite in a house overlooking Beacon Hill Park. I rented an apartment a couple of doors down, though I spent most of my time at her place. Our landlord, Ferdinand Mundigler, an outwardly stern but kind man, lived a couple of doors in the other direction. One day he bumped into me on the sidewalk, with a mattress on my back, moving my stuff into Patty's place. We rewrote the rental agreement with Ferdinand, putting my name on it too, gave notice at my apartment and suddenly we were living together. Actually it wasn't so sudden; we had essentially been already.

I hit it off immediately with Patty's family. Her father, Ron Moores, was a lovely man, the kind of dad or father-in-law whose support you can always count on. He was a firefighter who had retired just before I met Pat. And he had a great sense of humour. "Ronzie" was a navy veteran who'd survived a hurricane on a weathership in the north Pacific. His abiding faith and positive outlook was forged in his own difficult upbringing. Handsome and always impeccably groomed, Ron was a true gentlemen, and I couldn't have been blessed with a better father-in-law. Her mother, Katie, was a character. She had immigrated to Canada from England in 1948, after a career as a nurse and midwife in London. She used to ride her bike around the city during the Blitz, delivering babies. She had come to Canada to help her sister, a war bride who was raising a young family. Katie could be a handful, but she was kind and loving and enjoyed the fact that I was on television. It always seemed to come up, even in conversation with strangers.

I also clicked immediately with Patty's brother, Barry, who is one of the funniest, quickest wits I have ever known, and who has become one of my best friends. He is hilarious. And he's extremely loyal, the kind of guy who has your back and would do anything for you. At the time, Barry was single, after a divorce from his first wife. He was seeing a woman he'd later marry, Jill. She was a loans officer at a bank, and as it turned out, by coincidence, I had just met her a short time before when I was applying for a car loan. Did I mention bad credit?

Patty's BFF Debby was also in a new relationship. She was dating a former hockey player named Dave Ross, who had returned to Victoria after a stellar major junior hockey career that had taken him to the NHL and the Los Angeles Kings. Dave is an outstanding guy who also quickly became one of my best friends. He is a riot, loves to tell and listen to stories and is a master chef— not officially, but he should be. Big D, as we call him, is the best cook I know. In fact, I always thought if I ever wrote a book it would be my favourite recipes (of his).

The three couples spent a lot of time together socially then, and we still do today.

Debby and Dave were the first to get engaged, and for me that meant the heat was on, though I needed no convincing. Patty and I are perfect for each other, and it didn't take me long to figure that out. My mom always said we made a good team and she was right.

So, I bought an engagement ring and was ready to pop the question around Christmas 1987. We had all stayed at Barry's house on Christmas Eve, and I think Patty had an inkling. I lavished her with gifts, but she was intent on finding a ring-sized box under the tree. The closest she came was a Chia Pet, the hot new thing in the day, which was the smallest wrapped package from me she could find. It was literally tossed over her shoulder when she opened it and found it didn't sparkle. There was no way I was putting an engagement ring under the Christmas tree. Too public.

I could sense she was a little disappointed, but maybe intrigued, as we went back to our Beacon Hill apartment. I had to get ready to work. We had a newscast Christmas Day, and being relatively new at the station, and single, I offered to take the shift so the people with young families could have the holiday off.

Before I left, as we sat in the living room, I proposed. But I didn't go down on one knee. Don't ask me why. If I had it to do again, I would genuflect until the cows came home. Even without that touch, it was still an amazing moment. Patty is a hopeless romantic; she imagines wind blowing in her hair and music playing a soundtrack in the background. I hope this met her expectation. But it didn't help that I had to leave in an hour for work, if only for a half-shift.

We were married on the lawn of the Deep Cove Chalet in North Saanich on September 3, 1988. It was the hottest day of the year. Patty's dad had been in the hospital but was released on that day to walk her down the aisle and give her away. My brother Gary was my best man. Debby's dad, Roy, an accomplished musician in the Naden military band, played the wedding march on his trumpet. The venue could not have been more beautiful, and the ceremony and reception were even more perfect. In my toast from the head table, I forgot to mention my dad. I wish I had.

Gary did a great job emceeing the wedding reception inside the chalet, and it will always be one of my favourite memories of him. The food was great, and the room was lovely. Patty was a beautiful bride, wearing a dress that had been to the altar a couple of times already. It was Debby's mom's wedding dress, with a few alterations.

It was a daytime event, so there was no dancing after the mid-afternoon luncheon. People still talk about the food, the kind of spread for which chef Pierre Koffel is renowned. But Patty and I were long gone before it was all over. We'd arranged for a helicopter to land on the lawn after the reception and fly us to the airport in Vancouver for a flight to Los Angeles and a wedding night at the Beverly Hills Hotel. The helicopter was déjà vu for Gary and his wife, Jo-Jo, who flew away from their Detroit wedding in one. Theirs was a nod to her airborne traffic reporting. In our case, we weren't copying; it really was the only way we'd make it to Vancouver in time for our flight. And it was a pretty cool way to make an exit.

Our original honeymoon plan had been a cruise, but earlier in the year we'd cancelled that when we had the opportunity to buy a house, a mid-century bungalow (as they would call it on house hunting shows these days) in Saanich near the University of Victoria. We still live here today. It's a sleeper from the street, but it has a lovely private backyard with a swimming pool. We've made some changes over the years, but not many since moving in, in April of 1988.

Deb and Dave got married in May of that same year, ahead of us by a few months. Barry and Jill married the following year, and they were the first of our group to start having children. We were third out of the gate amongst our friends and family. Barry and Jill had already had their first, our nephew David, and Deb and Dave had had a daughter, Emily, all within the preceding year. In the summer of 1991, Patty and I discovered we were expecting. Rachel was born in January the following year. Our eldest son, Hamilton, arrived a year later in August, two days after Debby and Dave's son, Adrian. The pregnancies were practically in sync. Everything we three couples did seemed to be in near unison, including maternity. Until we were the only ones out of the three couples to have a third baby. Our son Sheldon was born in September 1996.

Barry and Jill also have a daughter, Sarah, who was born two months before Hamilton. Barry's daughter from his first marriage, Christy, died suddenly in 1995 at the age of thirteen. We still miss her. Christy lived with her mom in Ladysmith, and she was hiking up a trail along a power line on the hillside near their home when she collapsed. Her friend ran for help, but when paramedics arrived they couldn't save her. She had suffered from an undiagnosed heart condition. Christy was a sweetheart. She used to call me Uncle Hut. For all of us new parents, she was our first. I will always have a place in my heart for her.

They say there is no name for being a parent who has lost a child, because it is simply too horrible. Barry and Jill, and Christy's mom, Julie, all showed incredible strength through the tragedy. Christy would be proud, especially of her dad. Losing her gave me better insight into what my own parents had gone through before I was born.

Christy's death came just three months after my brother's, and just weeks before Patty was in a serious car accident. She totalled our van in Burnaby on her way to a weekend workshop while she was getting her real estate licence. Fortunately, she was okay. The year 1995 was horrible for us, but it proved once again the strength and resilience of the human spirit. You can get through this.

Watching your children grow and become individuals on their own is one of life's great pleasures. There is nothing that makes me prouder than being their father.

How lucky I am to be their dad. And how lucky I am to be married to Patty. She is a star.

Pat had been hired at CHEK after a number of other jobs and a move to Vancouver. And she got the job she wanted at CHEK as a production assistant, despite not having previous formal training for that position. From a PA she pushed herself to become a producer and director, but she didn't put her career before her family.

After Sheldon was born, Patty stepped away from television to devote herself to raising our children. But she didn't give up on her ambition and worked through that difficult year for our family, in 1995, to earn her real estate licence. Circumstances at CHEK at the time forced her to let her licence lapse, but she stayed in the realty industry, thriving as a partner to a classmate and friend, Lee Johnston, who has become one of Greater Victoria's leading realtors.

In the last couple of years, since rewriting her real estate exam and earning her licence again, Patty has grown once more, and is herself thriving as a realtor. And it is thanks to her knowledge and smarts that we have been able to accumulate a stable of rental properties in our neighbourhood, four houses in addition to our own.

She always wanted to host a radio show, to use it to help others and share knowledge and understanding. And she has done that, too. *Lifestyle with Patty Mack*, Saturdays on C-FAX in Victoria, has earned a dedicated listener following and is a venue for experts and everyday people to share what they know, to help people live a good lifestyle and enjoy their life. "Enjoy" is a word Patty loves to use, and it's a touchstone in the way she lives her life.

Her latest passion is buying and restoring old vanities, then giving them away to women, both young and old, who can use a little inspiration. A makeup table is just the thing to give such a boost. Keep an eye out for "The Vanity Project." It's going to be big.

There is nothing my wife cannot do that she sets her mind to. And usually what she sets her mind to is finding a way to be a positive influence in someone's life, a way to make a difference. I love her dearly and couldn't be more proud of her. Same goes for our kids.

Patty is a hopeless romantic, and my first foray into writing came early in our relationship, when I started a novel called *Patty's Story*. I never finished it and it was pretty syrupy stuff, but it came straight from the heart. I think those yellowed old typewritten pages are in a hope chest somewhere.

When her parents celebrated their twenty-fifth wedding anniversary many years ago, they had a ceremony to renew their vows. I might have known, standing on the lawn on September 3, 1988, that this was something we'd be doing too, in a quarter-century. How the time flies. In 2013, just a few days before our actual anniversary, we held a silver anniversary ceremony of our own, renewing our vows with our children, Rachel, Hamilton and Sheldon, there as our witnesses, on a beach in Maui. Patty had wanted this so much, and I'm so glad she did, because she made it happen. It was an afternoon none of us will ever forget, as we dedicated ourselves to each other, again.

If it's possible to love Patty even more now than I did then, I do. She is the love of my life and I'm a very lucky guy.

# 5
# Family Time

There is no greater joy in my life than my family, Patty and our kids. We have enjoyed good health and a happy home filled with fun and laughter. There's been some hollering too, but what house with three little kids hasn't heard that?

We have never moved from the home in Saanich we bought the year we got married. Patty and I have never really wanted to, and the kids were always adamantly against it. The only place that I really thought would be worth the upheaval was about a kilometre away overlooking Cadboro Bay. But is a view worth upsetting the apple cart and sparking rebellion in your children? We didn't think so.

Our kids are died-in-the-wool traditionalists, especially Hamilton. Maybe they get that from their mom, who's a Taurus and resistant to change (although she is getting better with that). One of our family traditions, maybe the biggest, is travelling together. It's getting harder, though, coordinating the work and university schedules of these young adults. That's why trips together these days are even more special.

For years, more than twenty, in fact, we would make our annual summer pilgrimage from Victoria to Calgary to visit my family, when Leilani and my mom were still alive. It's something Patty and I had already done for years before the kids were born. And in those early days without children, we'd sometimes come home with a pet. Twice we stopped at a farmhouse in Monte Creek, east of Kamloops, lured off the highway by the big spray-painted plywood sign at the side of the road: KITTENS. That's how we got Cindy, and the next year Betty. Don't ask me how we decided to give cats human names. Those two cats are long gone, their place now taken by Linda and Mr. Butterscotch (the kids got to name him).

There are as many pets as people at our house. In addition to the two old cats, we also have three dogs. Sophie is our Airedale terrier, who has been part of the family for nearly fourteen years now. We've since added two more dogs to our menagerie, both Chihuahua crosses, both rescues. Taco is a cross with a miniature Italian greyhound, so she is Chihuahua sized with a greyhound's body and snout, long legs and blinding speed. We've had her for three years, and that was by accident too.

We'd done a quick story on the newscast one Friday night, about a local group bringing in about twenty dogs from a high-kill shelter in California. Patty and I were discussing it over a glass of wine that evening and, to my surprise, she suggested we get one.

"What would we call it?" I asked.

"Taco!" she said.

I love dogs, pretty much all dogs, and always have. But in truth, I was never really a small-dog guy. That changed with Taco, and she has taken years off Sophie, who has been slowing down and getting pretty stiff, with a sore lower back and arthritic hips. They play like little kids.

We are coming up on the first anniversary of our latest, and maybe last, addition to our animal kingdom. Patty came across an online ad from another rescue group of an adorable little

Chihuahua, this one crossed with a Dachshund, what's called a "Cheweenie," I'm told. Zuzu (as in the little girl with the cold in *It's a Wonderful Life*) has been another great addition, though she's a little neurotic.

Patty and I now understand how couples, as they get older, gravitate to small dogs and baby them. We're there. And yes, we do have outfits for them. Sweaters, mostly, and a couple of Hallowe'en costumes. We'll be the ones with two Chihuahuas on the dashboard of the RV. Maybe it's the empty nest syndrome. And we're almost there, too.

When people tell you to savour each minute with your children when they're little, make sure you listen. Because you don't know they are right until you are looking back on those years. I have never held that couples must have children to be fulfilled and happy, but I can't imagine life without Rachel, Hamilton and Sheldon. They are truly a blessing—and how proud we are of each of them.

Rachel was born in January 1992. The birth of your first child is an experience like no other. When Patty was due, her doctor helped get labour started in her office, with what I can only guess is the physician's equivalent of a crochet hook. We went straight to Victoria General, and the contractions had started by the time we got to the labour and delivery ward.

There's nothing like the feeling of excitement and fear, even though we figured we knew what we were doing. We'd attended Lamaze classes, where the breathing practice and stretching was punctuated by expectant young moms expelling flatus. Patty called me out one time, but it wasn't me. Really.

After several hours of labour for Patty, all of it captured on home video (did I ever edit that down?), push came to shove, literally. Everything was fine, but the baby wasn't moving through the final stretch. Patty's doctor called in the attending obstetrician for a forceps delivery. Before long, the room, which for hours had been dark and private, was bathed in light and full of white lab coats. They could have set up stadium seating. Now I know why they say a woman's modesty disappears as soon as she's had a baby.

While the OB/GYN set up shop, the attending pediatrician was chatting with me, though I couldn't focus on small talk. He was a lovely man, and a great doctor, but at the moment he seemed a little star-struck. He knew me from television, and he was telling me about all of the other notable public figures who'd been through his delivery room. I wasn't really interested. I was fixated instead on the big forceps the other doctor was getting ready to insert into my wife, with which to pull out my baby by the head. They looked like giant gleaming salad tongs. I adjusted the video camera.

The attending physician knew what he was doing, thank goodness, because within a minute he had brought our baby girl into the world. Rachel arrived with a couple of "stork bites," little bruises from the forceps, which faded fast. She had an exotic look to her, accentuated by a head of bushy, dark brown hair.

By comparison, the birth of Hamilton in August of the following year was more sedate. Again, all three couples were in sync. Barry and Jill had welcomed our niece Sarah in June, and Debby was in labour almost simultaneously with Patty. While Deb was in, we kept going to the hospital, thinking "it was time," but twice we mistook a gush of water from our swimming pool for ruptured amniotic fluid. (The chlorine was a dead giveaway.)

Ham was effortless in delivery (at least as far as I was concerned; Patty might tell another version). Everything went smoothly, and the pain of childbirth was managed by the magic of an epidural anesthetic. Hammy was the quietest, most serene newborn you could imagine.

It was standing room only during visiting hours though. Debby had given birth to Adrian two days earlier, and before either of them was discharged to take home their new baby boys, there was a party atmosphere in the maternity ward.

Sheldon was the fastest arrival of the three, and the biggest too. By now we were the only ones in our group still having babies. We'd thought about four, but Patty has always liked the number three. When the time came, we felt like old hands at this. It's true you get a little more used to the process and know what to expect.

When we got to the hospital, he was already on his way, and this would be our (do you like that, "our"?) first natural delivery. Not by choice, there just wasn't time to get the anesthetist. Sheldon arrived after less than a couple of hours' labour, clocking in at an even ten pounds, bigger than his brother or sister, almost like a toddler already. He also had huge hands for a newborn, and prophetically we said he looked like a football player, even on his first day.

Our three kids have always been close and are good friends today, even though they have begun to go their separate ways. When they were little, the boys shared a room with bunk beds after Rachel graduated to her own bedroom. But they liked it better together and would often plot to drag Rachel's double mattress to the floor of the boys' room, something they've still done on Christmas Eve until lately.

As I said, they love family traditions and none more so than around Christmas. It's funny the things you do that get ingrained, from your childhood to your children's. *It's a Wonderful Life, Elf*, and *Miracle on 34th Street*. A DVD of an old Bing Crosby/Frank Sinatra Christmas Special. Must-see holiday viewing. Not *A Christmas Story* so much; the scene with the kid's tongue frozen to the light pole freaked them out when they were little.

We have always gone to church on Christmas Eve, followed by Chinese food with family and one of those movies, usually *It's a Wonderful Life*. The turkey dinner was often at our place, and Patty's dad, Ron—or "Ronzie" as we called him (a nickname from his fire hall days)—would perform an after-dinner tradition known as The Wry Face Family. He could contort his face and screw up his mouth in such a way that no member of The Wry

Face Family could put out the Christmas candle until the baby turned it upside down. This was a delight for everyone at the table. A childhood dinner tradition for Sheldon was the turkey drumstick, as big as he was some years.

Over the years, Sunday dinners with family became a tradition the kids enjoyed. We'd have Patty's folks, Ron and Katie, over, not quite every week, but close. And unless it was barbecue season, Sunday dinner was usually roast beef and Yorkshire pudding. I'm not sure if the Yorkshires were as good as Katie said she used to have in England, but the gravy usually turned out pretty well. They all encourage me to bottle and sell it, but I'm not sure about that. My own mom taught me how to make gravy many years ago, and you know what they say about practice. (The secret is in the roux.)

We've shared that Sunday roast with friends and family, and other meals on a Saturday night, usually with our circle, Debby and Dave, and Barry and Jill. We are fortunate to have close family and best friends with whom we are so compatible, with a shared notion of having fun.

Travelling with our kids is something that we have made a tradition since they were born. We'd rather not go on trips unless our children are with us, though there have been some by necessity.

Many of our family trips have been taken in our old RV, "the MoHo." There are newer, fancier and bigger motorhomes, but I couldn't be happier than when I am in ours, with Patty and the kids, and the dogs. Getting somewhere and setting up the camp, transforming a spot on the side of the road, or in a Walmart parking lot, into a little piece of paradise. For years it seems we celebrated every one of Hamilton's birthdays in the MoHo, since we were usually on the road in late August, often dragging our boat behind it.

Many of our best summer holiday memories are in the MoHo, but not all. One of the most memorable was a motor trip across Canada in the summer of 2001. I had three weeks' vacation that year, even though that's a long time to be off the air. We drove an Aerostar van at the time and made the usual trek over the Rockies to Calgary, dawdling as we went. Once we got there, after a few days at my sister's, we decided to head east.

We travelled from Calgary to Peggys Cove, Nova Scotia, and back, in fifteen days. That's a round-trip distance of about ten thousand kilometres. And this was before iPads and video screens in the headrests. Somehow our kids kept themselves entertained while seeing the country. There were many long days on the road. And long nights, too, like a sweltering overnight at a truck stop in Eau Claire, Wisconsin. We slept in the van because there were no motels open when we got there. (Actually, we slept in the van a lot, if it was too late to set up our tent, or if we couldn't find the luxury of a cabin at a KOA campground.)

When we woke in Eau Claire, amidst the idling transport trucks, we hit the road before sunrise and drove for sixteen hours straight before calling it a night in Indian Head, Saskatchewan. The owner of the KOA in that prairie town agreed to open the swimming pool, because I'd been promising the kids a swim since noon. Good people in Saskatchewan. Hours earlier, Hammy had burst into tears when we opened a window in the van and the wind sucked out the roadmap from his lap; the kids had traced out our entire route on it. That souvenir from our holiday ended up in a ditch by an interstate, somewhere in Minnesota or North Dakota.

I think our kids were used to those long driving trips from the annual visit to Calgary. We'd always stop at the halfway point in Salmon Arm, usually at a campground on Shuswap Lake. And the stopover would include a visit to a local cheese plant, a fruit stand, a tour of my old teenage haunts, and always a visit to my dad's gravesite in the Mount Ida Cemetery, with a picture each year as the kids got bigger.

We can't count the number of times these kids have been to Disneyland, starting from a very early age, when we drove with

Rachel in a car seat. We thought if we kept shovelling bottles of juice and milk at her, it would keep her quiet. The only thing that did was a Barney cassette that played on a continuous loop. She loved Barney, except the year her Uncle Barry rented a Barney costume for her birthday party. She was terrified. The same thing happened when I was dressed as the Easter Bunny another year.

One Disney trip stands out, when the kids were in their late teens. We had to layover in Los Angeles overnight en route to my favourite holiday spot, Zihuatanejo, Mexico. Our connecting flight via Seattle had been cancelled, so what should have been almost a full day in the Magic Kingdom was reduced to a little over an hour before the park closed at midnight. And we'd never have made it if not for an LA cabbie doing a hundred miles an hour down the Santa Ana Freeway.

There was another Disney trip where the memories started long before we saw Mickey or Minnie. Sheldon was a baby, still little enough not to need his own seat on the plane. We thought it would be a good idea to add some gripe water to his baby bottle, but it did anything but soothe him. As soon as we were airborne, I was walking the aisle of the plane, trying to settle him, but he was out of control. The Air Canada crew told me to sit down, but before I could, he threw his bottle, which exploded in a man's lap a few rows back. I've been patient with parents on planes ever since. The flight attendant made a point of telling another passenger, in a voice deliberately loud enough for Patty and me to hear, "I can't understand why people take babies to Disneyland." I can.

We've done it all with these kids: the West Coast and Oregon Dunes (highly recommend it); a fly-and-drive from San Francisco to LA and back (made notable by the creepy drifter who was stalking our niece Sarah in the SFO airport, and Hammy and me nearly getting robbed at a gas station), and a fly-and-drive along the Gulf Coast.

That trip was a few years ago, and it was inspired by the boys' high school football careers and their love of the movie *Friday*

*Night Lights.* We flew to New Orleans and drove to South Padre Island, Texas, before veering north and west to Odessa, home of the Permian High School Panthers, made famous in the book and the movie—and inspiration for the TV show. Do you know anyone else who would drive twenty-five hundred miles across west Texas to see a high school football stadium? We did. And we sampled Texas hospitality, thanks to a family in a burger joint (Whataburger, check it out if you're in Texas—it's almost as good as Dick's in Seattle). They overheard us trying to figure out where to find the school, or somewhere to buy team souvenirs. Not only did they give us directions, they tracked us down at the local mall, after calling a coach to open the school and training facility on a Saturday night so the boys could see it. Nice people in Texas.

That trip ended in Dallas, and before we flew home I got to scratch off an entry on my bucket list: visiting Dealey Plaza, where JFK was assassinated. I've had a lifelong fascination with the Kennedy assassination, and it was a wish of mine to see where it happened. I am not a conspiracy nut, but am not convinced that what we've been told is exactly what happened that day.

After Ronzie died, Patty's mom, Katie, took all of us and Barry and Jill and their kids on a cruise to Alaska. It was Katie's last big trip after a lifetime of travel. Our kids had only been on one other cruise, but Patty and I have been fortunate to take many.

For several years, Patty and I escorted travel groups on cruises around the world. It came about almost by accident, after another CHEK on-air host was scheduled to host a Mediterranean trip in the early 1990s, when Rachel and Hamilton were babies. I was opposed to it, until he left for another station and the cruise landed in our lap.

That was the first of many cruises, including Scandinavia and St. Petersburg, Russia. That itinerary included a stop in Berlin, shortly after reunification. We've also escorted groups through the Panama Canal and the Mexican Riviera, which is how we discovered Zihuatanejo.

Our second group cruise in the Mediterranean came in 2000, but our two stops in Israel were scrubbed because of the violence and fighting, which was triggered by Prime Minister Ariel Sharon's visit to the Temple Mount. The night before we were to dock in Ashdod, the captain announced it was too dangerous. That was a disappointment. I've always wanted to visit Israel. Earlier on that trip we got a taste of the tension in the region, with extreme security for our visit to the pyramids in Egypt.

Patty and I were very fortunate to have had the opportunity to take so many great trips, and at a young age. The only downside was that the kids couldn't come.

It wasn't always uneventful while we were away. Once we were greeted at the airport by the kids with their babysitter and discovered Rachel with a broken arm. And it wasn't the first time she'd been in a cast. She'd suffered a leg fracture in the playground in Beacon Hill Park when she was younger. And Sheldon had been in a cast for a break when he was little too.

That paled in comparison to the break Shel suffered in high school, and it happened on the football field. He was in Grade 11 and was coming off a breakout season for the Mount Doug Rams. He'd been a standout in the provincial AAA championship game, after moving to the middle linebacker position, and was already being recruited by a number of universities. It was the last day of the spring camp, and he'd gone down funny on a tackle during practice. He'd suffered a serious fracture of his tibia and fibula and needed surgery, which left him on crutches for the whole summer. But he showed real character in the face of adversity, and was back to play after missing the first couple of games in the next season that fall.

It was a bad break, but not as gross as the open compound tib-fib break that Patty suffered the weekend of her fortieth birthday, and Sheldon was part of that too, still a baby. She was carrying him down our front stairs to go to the Victoria Day Parade. She lost her balance, fell forward, and it was her mother's instinct to protect her child that made her twist around as she went down. It snapped her leg above the ankle, the broken bone sticking through her shin. It took months of recovery and a titanium rod, but she's as good as new, though it hurts more than I think she lets on. Ronzie was the Rock of Gibraltar that day for us, just as he was for Barry when they got the terrible news about Christy. Ron was a great man, and the strength of his character was forged in a difficult childhood and upbringing.

Sheldon's broken leg healed by fall, and he was champing at the bit to get on the field again. We were on pins and needles during his first game, worried about the leg. But we didn't need to be. An opposing player stepped on his hand during the game, breaking a finger. He played with it like that for the rest of the season; the hand and leg are just fine. And after weighing his options, Sheldon accepted a football scholarship from the University of British Columbia. Sheldon has now completed his first year at university, working towards an Arts degree, and his first season on the UBC Thunderbirds.

Sheldon is a gentle giant, big and broad, and like Hamilton, he now towers over the Old Man in stature and strength. But beneath that brawn is a gentle soul who is thoughtful and kind, though he tries to look tough. Shel will always be the baby of the family, but he is an old soul, wise beyond his years. And though he may be the last person to ask for help, he's the first to offer a hand or go out of his way for others.

Sheldon had followed his brother's footsteps onto the football field at Mount Douglas Secondary. Hamilton played football first in Grade 9 and again in Grade 12, as well as basketball and soccer, among others. He loves and excels at all sports and is a natural athlete. Since graduation he's been working toward a degree in Political Science and Economics at the University of Victoria, but his true love is sports, and that passion will likely lead him into a sports management career of some kind. Hamilton is a walking encyclopedia (has Google made that term quaint?), with knowledge and facts at his fingertips on any subject you might bring up. But it's particularly his knowledge of sports, and his keen interest, that makes it a natural choice for him. I think he would also be a great broadcaster, and I know that interests him too, though I've never pushed him or any of the kids to follow in the family business.

Hamilton likes to let on that he's a hard nut to crack, but he is kind, compassionate and sensitive, and always willing to do anything for you. He cares about people. Ham has a wicked sense of humour, and he is and always was a character. For years when he was little, it was difficult to get a family photo without Hammy making a silly face. He would sign off his work for much of elementary school as Batman, and for what felt like years would wear only a T-shirt with the dark knight's logo. He never did and still won't wear a coat and will never admit to being cold. It was his opposition to clothing that caused a stir on a summer holiday in Salmon Arm one year. What happened was part of a hellish holiday that has become family legend.

But it wasn't one of the old wagons that featured in these holiday hijinks. It was my 1977 Cadillac Seville. I loved that car. It was a bit of a beater, too, though you'd never know to look at it. Silver with a landau roof, spokes and every luxury known to Cadillac in the late 1970s. I still think the style of the Seville is classic. This was actually Patty's brother Barry's Seville, which I had bought from him after selling my first one, which I always thought was nicer. In any event, the car was not adequate for the task at hand: towing an overloaded thirty-five-hundred-pound tent trailer over the steep climb of the Coquihalla Highway in thirty-five-degree heat, with two children under the age of four and a wife who was eight months' pregnant.

We didn't make it up the first big hill before the radiator blew. After waiting all day for repair, we hit the road again, only to blow a tire. Back to the shop, where we had to get two so they'd match, and on the highway again. Almost to the top of the hill and the toll booth (still there then), and the rad hose now split because the newly repaired radiator had increased the pressure in the system.

I did a "MacGyver" on the hose, and we kept going. By now it was getting dark; it had been almost twelve hours since we set out, and we hadn't even made it to the town of Merritt. As it got darker and darker, I hoped in vain for the lights of the town over every horizon, not daring to tell Patty that the gas tank was now on empty and the warning light had been blinking for several kilometres.

Finally, we filled up and got to the Shuswap campsite, where we were meeting Barry and Jill and their kids for several days of camping together. I put up our tent trailer at 2:00 AM as Rachel woke the campground with her screaming: "We're here!"

In the morning, we discovered our food had gone bad because the fridge was off the whole way during the previous day's repairs and heat. After breakfast, Barry and Jill announced they'd decided to head for Banff the next day. We headed into town to buy a radiator hose and groceries and discovered that our bank card was declined because there'd been a problem with the payday deposit. By the afternoon, that was all sorted, and we had the hose, fresh food, ice for the cooler and, mercifully, cold beer. Back at the beach at the private campsite, we were finally settling in. Patty, pregnant and out to here, was finally able to relax in the sand while the kids played on the beach. A good time for me to run up to the trailer and reload my beverage. It just couldn't have ended so well.

On the way back, I was accosted by the campsite owner, whose kid I had known in high school, demanding that I make my son wear a bathing suit or we'd be kicked out.

"We've had complaints."

"Complaints?" I barked. "Who in a family campground complains about a two-year-old boy naked at the lake?"

"Get him dressed, or you're out!"

You might be able to guess what happened after that. I told Henry, remembering his name, to go forward and procreate, or words to that effect. Once the yelling had died down, I marched down to the beach to break the news to Patty.

"Pack up your stuff. We're out of here."

Again, you might be able to guess what's next. More yelling. Some crying. Me turning the air blue with a string of profane invective as I hastily tore down the tent trailer. To add comic relief for our fellow campers (but not for me), one of the struts on the trailer would not crank down, so the trailer looked like some bizarre carnival attraction with one corner sticking up, canvas flapping in the wind as we roared off in the Seville. We ditched the trailer in my friend's yard and limped to Calgary, where we hunkered down at Leilani's place for the rest of the vacation. If only Hammy would have worn a bathing suit.

I can pull up similarly themed holiday tales involving Rachel as well. I don't think she was even two when she realized she could exercise control over the adults.

We were on our way home from Calgary one summer, with my mom coming back to Victoria with us, and Rachel was in her car seat in the middle up front. My mom loved to visit when we would get together each year, and there was lots of chatter during the several hours of driving west. At least there was, until Rachel had heard enough.

"Stop talking to my daddy!" she demanded.

It came out "totting," and at first it seemed kind of cute. That is, until my mom tried to say another word.

Before she could utter a peep, Rachel would scream, "STOP TOTTING TO MY DADDY!"

We made it to Penticton before stopping for the night, again with a tent trailer. By the time we got there, we felt like we'd been beaten up, and all we wanted was a swim in Skaha Lake. But a roaring windstorm had blown in and we couldn't get the trailer set up. We needed a drink after that drive, and I mixed up some therapeutic gin and tonics in the only thing at our disposal, Rachel's baby bottles. I'll never forget Patty and my mom and me splashing around in the wind and the waves, drinking gin through a nipple.

Rachel was always a character, even from a very early age. She used to ride her trike around inside the house, wearing white gloves and cowboy boots. She wrote a protest letter when the local 7-Eleven store increased the price of its penny candy. And she has always been a very loyal friend. She puts a high value on friendship and always finds time for the people she cares about, even at her own expense. She may have learned a lesson, though, when she organized her own birthday party. I think she was turning eleven or maybe twelve, and she wanted as many girls for a sleepover as we could manage. I think we cut it off at eighteen. I suspect she thought more guests equals more presents. But the party was a disaster and before bedtime she was in tears and wanted it to be over.

Rachel has always had an incredible work ethic. She puts in long hours and devotes a lot of effort to anything she sets her mind to. She is currently studying abroad, working toward her Master of Global Business Degree, after earning her Bachelor of Commerce from the Gustavson School of Business at the University of Victoria. She's been attending university in Rouen, France, since the fall, and has now completed her term in Seoul, South Korea. She'll be back in Victoria this summer before setting off again on an internship before getting her postgraduate degree.

Rachel is kind and generous, and she is sensitive. But she doesn't suffer fools, and she expects others to hit the targets she sets for herself.

The neat thing about our children is that although we have fortunately been able to take them places and give them many experiences and opportunities, they do not have a notion of entitlement. They have been good kids who have grown into responsible, thriving young adults. They are good citizens. We could not be prouder of them. I can think of nothing that matters as much, nor gives me more pleasure and pride, than our family life and our children.

Don't worry if it goes by quickly, because they do grow up fast. Enjoy every minute of it; the best is yet to come.

# 6

## Leilani

As I write this, it is four years to the day since my sister, Leilani, died. I was at her bedside in the Rockyview Hospital in Calgary on that cold November night. Her husband, Jim, was down the hall having a quick nap in the lounge. I was watching the Stampeders CFL football game beside the bed on the tiny hospital TV and was on the verge of dozing off myself. But I wasn't really asleep and kept an ear to her laboured breathing. When the room went silent, I was jolted out of my seat. I knew it was coming and it was a relief in the end—that's such a cliché, but it's true. Her suffering was finally over.

I'd been there since early that morning. Her husband and daughter, Elizabeth, had called me the night before when she was taken to the hospital, short of breath. It was too late to get a flight from Victoria, so I flew out as early as I could the next morning. We knew that this was likely the end.

Leilani was living with stage-four lung cancer. The diagnosis had come earlier that year, in the summer of 2010. She was in the Tom Baker Cancer Centre at Calgary's Foothills Hospital, the same place my dad had been in 1973. A ward clerk inadvertently told me she had an inoperable tumour as I was leaving the floor for my flight back to Victoria, even before doctors had broken the news to her.

Everyone always asks, "Did she smoke?" as though this is some comfort to know that getting sick was an inevitability, and her own fault. The fact is, she did smoke, quite heavily for most of her life, and had done so since her teens. But so what? She knew she should quit. My mom used to do everything she could to help her try to quit. She lived with a certain amount of self-loathing over it. But it was something she enjoyed in her life. And it did not define her.

In the end, as it turned out, it was not smoking that caused her cancer. Leilani had endured a lifetime of health issues and illness, and in her final days, I think she was just sick to death of it. Pun intended. She had suffered a heart attack earlier, I suspect brought on by the unintended stress of having our elderly mother move into their Calgary home. Leilani was fifty-two when she died.

She had lived with lupus for years and had beaten cancer twice previously. She was diagnosed with Hodgkin's disease in the early 1990s and beat it the first time with chemotherapy and radiation. But it came back several years later, and when she underwent another round of radiation bombardment, her oncologist warned that one side effect could be a malignant tumour years later: liver, lung or kidney, maybe in ten or fifteen years. And so it was, almost to the day, that the lung cancer diagnosis came. Though it may have been cold comfort, she found some solace in the knowledge that the type of small-cell cancer in her lungs was not the type brought on by years of cigarettes, but instead was the result of the earlier treatment.

Leilani was a little less than two years older than me. She and I were a second start for our parents and Gary, after Darrel died, although I know she was planned and I wasn't. She and I had always been close. We walked to and from school together in Calgary, and we stayed best friends when we were older, especially after we moved to Salmon Arm in 1971.

We grew up in an upper-middle-class neighbourhood in Calgary, in what is currently referred to as the Marda area. We just called it Southwest in those days. It's now quite a desirable part of the city, close in compared to the parts of Calgary that now stretch beyond the horizon in all directions. It was the usual upbringing. Then in Salmon Arm, we made new friends and settled in, though for the longest time she insisted on getting a ride to school, which was just a short walk away. She missed Calgary and she missed her old pals. Over the next couple of years, we would make many trips over the Rogers Pass to Calgary—as a family or by ourselves as teenagers on the Greyhound bus, which was great adventure.

I'm not sure that she ever loved Salmon Arm the way I came to. I think our father's death in 1974—she was sixteen and I was fourteen—had a different effect on each of us. Though I am not overtly religious, I believe I am spiritual, and I was oddly accepting of what had happened to our family. She turned away from whatever religious feeling she'd had. How could a caring, benevolent God do this?

In high school and long after, Leilani and I stayed close, hanging out together. Our group of friends was mutual and we did most of the same things. She dated and had several boyfriends, all of whom I liked—with maybe one or two exceptions. Leilani didn't finish high school, so she attended the local community college to complete her Grade 12 diploma. She was smart, but after our dad died, she may have lost her motivation a bit. I guess I did too. All this despite our mom's best efforts.

Leilani's health had been an issue since her teens. She had inherited from my dad's side an underslung jaw. It was not so severe as to affect her good looks but did cause a problem with her bite and would have led to dental issues. She had surgery at Vancouver General Hospital in the late 1970s. (I was back in Calgary at that point and flew to Vancouver to surprise her, then drove her and our mom back to Salmon Arm.) The surgery involved removing two pieces of jawbone and pushing the entire lower jaw back a few centimetres. It was then wired shut for several weeks to heal. On the drive home, we stopped at a McDonald's in Kamloops (they still didn't have one in Salmon Arm) and I taunted her with a Big Mac. I was just trying to be funny, but she burst into tears.

There was a complication from the surgery, an infection of sorts that may have been an encapsulation of TB picked up in the hospital. It was treated and got better and the jaw healed nicely. But in the aftermath of the operation, she developed what we later would realize was lupus, the autoimmune disorder in which the body essentially becomes allergic to itself. And it is manifested by an ache and malaise that she fought the rest of her life, though it did go into remission.

Leilani was brilliantly artistic. She could draw amazing portraits, and her childhood doodles were suitable for framing. She should have attended art school, and who knows where that might have taken her. Her artistic talent is still a highlight of the Christmas season for our family, as we hang the beautifully detailed and gorgeous needlepoint stockings she made for me and Patty and the kids.

She didn't go to art school but worked as a teller in a bank in Salmon Arm. That lasted a couple of years, but it was not really what she wanted. And she took a medical stenography course but didn't pursue that as a career either. She moved back to Calgary around the time I moved to Prince George in 1982, and she got an apartment with her old childhood best friend, Alicean Rutledge.

She worked at the Calgary Convention Centre, where she met Jim Harvie, whom she married on a bitterly cold, minus-forty-two-degree Calgary day, December 27, 1992. They had a daughter, my niece Elizabeth, who is an accomplished tuba player and, after considering a career in nursing, is now following in her uncle's footsteps, attending the journalism program at my alma mater,

SAIT. She'll be great. I am very proud of her, and I know Leilani is too. Growing up while her mom was sick was hard for Liz, and I know what she's been through, as she was almost the same age as me when we lost a parent. Jim has a new partner since Leilani died, and I'm glad. I know she would be too.

Leilani loved current events and the news. She loved to talk to me about it on the phone. She had a satellite dish so she could watch my newscast, and I'd get emails during the show with real time feedback about someone's grammar, or what a reporter was wearing, always in kindness. She was a stickler for the language, another Scrabble nut in our family. I doubt there is any family that has played more Scrabble than we did, though she later gravitated to Sudoku and computer games. I think it's probably a good thing Candy Crush didn't come along while she was alive.

And like me, she loved TV. In the days before PVRs, she would have three or four VCRs rolling at any given time. I'm not sure she ever watched all of the stuff she recorded.

Sometimes I can't write about Leilani or talk about her without getting a lump in my throat. She was brave and lived her life to the end with incredible grace. She was a caring daughter to our mom, and a loving mother herself, a dear friend and a wonderful sister. The only one I will ever have. And I miss her a lot.

# 7

# A Tale of Two Cities

If you've ever visited Prince George, or have ever lived there, you know it can seem to take a long time to get there. It doesn't just *seem* like a long time, it *is*. It's an eight- or nine-hour drive from Vancouver, depending on the weather and road conditions, and about the same, maybe a little less, to the next closest big city, Edmonton.

I had never been to Prince George at the time I decided, in 1982 at age twenty-two, to move there. My time had come to an end in Kamloops, where I had my first real job in broadcasting, two years after I had gotten my start. It may seem like an odd career move, but I'll explain later.

I had no idea what to expect, but when CKPG news director Peter Clemente called me to ask for a tape and then offered me a job, I thought I should go. I don't want to say I had soured on Kamloops. But I had soured on the bad union management relationship at my first station, CFJC. I learned later that maybe it was the station that had soured on me.

The first time I drove to Prince George, which was moving

day, I couldn't believe I wasn't there yet. Fortunately, it was in the summer. PG winters are legendary, and although I thought I'd seen it all, seasonally, in Calgary, the snow and the cold in central BC is a character builder.

If you are into the outdoors and recreation, PG is the place. Especially in the winter. Ice fishing and snowmobiling are big there. There are surprisingly good ski hills close in, and bigger ones a couple of hours away. And if you'd rather stay inside when it's cold, and drink, well, that's popular too. At least it was amongst my group.

Prince George can be a rough place, as well. It has a reputation, probably well earned. It is almost at the geographic centre of the province, and it serves a wide area. Its backbone is the forest industry, specifically pulp and paper. There were, at the time that I arrived, three pulp mills in town, triangulating the valley where most of the city, at least downtown and the old original Fort George, are located.

You do get used to the smell, the rotten-egg odour that emanates from the steam stacks at the pulp mills. There used to be a rumour that they shut down or at least turned down the emission scrubbers on the weekends. We never were able to prove that for a story. But I do remember it sometimes smelled worse on Saturdays and Sundays. I would occasionally cover weekend mornings on the radio at CKPG, and when I emerged in the afternoon, there was a greenish, sticky and stinky sulphuric film that had settled on my car during the eight-hour shift. I didn't like to think that was what we were breathing.

Prince George was a good news town, and it was a good place for somebody young like me to get lots of experience. I covered a general assignment beat in the morning, was on the radio desk in the early afternoon, and then prepared and anchored the supper-time TV newscast. Later that night I might go out to cover a city council or school board meeting. There is no substitute for experience.

The station was then located downtown in a converted auto body shop, with the TV studio at the rear of the building. There was a side entrance near the control room, leading from the parking lot separating the station from a Chinese restaurant next door. Security from the lobby was pretty tight, with a secondary entrance you needed to be buzzed through. I always thought that considering what had happened, the side door should be more secure too.

If Prince George had a reputation for violence, then CKPG's past was part of it. The station was the scene of an incident that would become one of the most tragic chapters of Canada's hockey story.

Brian "Spinner" Spencer was the pride of Fort St. James, a small backwoods town northwest of Prince George, about an hour or so away. Spencer was drafted by the Toronto Maple Leafs in 1969. The following year, in December 1970, he was called up by the Leafs to play in what would be his first game televised on *Hockey Night in Canada*. Toronto was taking on the Chicago Black Hawks, and Spencer had been chosen to be interviewed between periods.

He was so proud, he called his dad, Roy, in Fort St. James to be sure he watched. Roy Spencer drove to Prince George to get a new antenna. Invited friends over for drinks beforehand. This was a big deal in a small town, and *HNIC* was an even bigger deal then, long before cable delivered multiple games every night of the week.

When Roy turned on the game, carried by CBC affiliate CKPG, he didn't get to see his son. What he saw instead was the league's newest expansion team, the Vancouver Canucks, playing the California Golden Seals on a regional feed. In an alcohol-fuelled rage, Spencer drove the 135 kilometres back to Prince George, and he took his shotgun with him. He burst into the station and held the master control operator at gunpoint, demanding that the Toronto game be switched on. The operator complied, lucky to have had access to the other national feed. He wasn't hurt. The RCMP had been called and were waiting when Roy stepped out the side door into the parking lot. He was ordered to drop the gun. He fired two shots instead, wounding one of the Mounties. Officers returned fire, and the out-of-control hockey dad was dead. "Spinner" Spencer was told what happened after the game. He still played the following night.

What happened in the parking lot at CKPG was part of the player's violent life. After an eleven-year pro hockey career, Spencer descended into a life of drugs and violence and was shot to death himself in 1988 during a crack cocaine robbery in Florida.

Roy Spencer's siege had happened years before I or many of my co-workers had arrived at CKPG. But it was something we'd often talk about, especially when there was an unexpected buzz at the side door after hours, or if we were standing at the very spot in the parking lot where it had happened. The incident also said something about the old Prince George in the 1970s, and to an extent, the city as I found it in 1982.

We used to go to the bar a lot after work, and I was fond of some of the rundown and, shall we say, seedier establishments. Although I quit going to one of them.

The Columbus Hotel was notoriously rough. A real workingman's tavern. We were in there one night, a bunch of us from the station, when a big, burly, bearded man at the bar began motioning to me. He was huge, with massive hands sticking out from the sleeves of a tattered red flannel shirt. I assumed he was a fan who recognized me from television! He must want to meet me and perhaps buy me a beer. I jogged across the crowded pub to where he was standing at the bar.

"You fucker. You hate unions, don't you?"

Not what I was expecting.

"Uh, um, no. Not me, mister. I don't hate unions," I squeaked.

"No, I've seen you on the news talking shit about unions. You're an asshole."

It went on a little longer in that vein, punctuated with more F-bombs and increasingly menacing body language.

"You stay here while I take a piss," he said, before turning and staggering past the pool tables for the men's room.

You might have thought I'd been shot out of a cannon, as I ran out the front doors of the Columbus.

I didn't bother to get my coat, and I didn't stop to tell my friends I was leaving. They were actually quite concerned about what had happened to me. This was long before everyone had a phone in their pocket and could text or call. I made it home okay. And I never set foot in the Columbus again. I couldn't now if I wanted to. It burned to the ground a few years ago.

We used to spend a lot of time at the Simon Fraser Inn, conveniently located across the street from the station. We'd go there for lunch because they had a great baron of beef dip sandwich special every day. It would usually be accompanied by a cold pint. Can you believe we used to do this at work?

The kitchen worker at the carving station was, we assumed, a recent arrival to Prince George from Vietnam. He never told us. He never spoke. We extrapolated from the tag on his white chef's coat that his full name was Dan Van Tranh, and what he served us was known as a Dan Van Tranh San. We meant no disrespect.

It was not service with a smile. In fact, as Dan Van Tranh waited for your order, he would flash his big carving knife at you, with a look on his face that said he'd rather be disembowelling you than carving off a few nice slices from the medium-rare hip of beef.

One other dangerous thing about those sandwiches: the Simon Fraser had the hottest horseradish any of us had ever eaten. So naturally, we had a daily contest to see who could swallow the biggest spoonful on every bite. It was eye-watering, hair-standing-straight-up-on-the-back-of-your-neck stuff, washed down with cold beer, almost every lunch hour. Then we'd go back to work, fight the burning indigestion and prepare the day's news.

There was another character we met in that Simon Fraser pub. His name was Alf Yeske, and he did tricks. He became a bit of a pet of ours, joining us in the evening, amusing us with his strange parlour games. Alf had been a lineman for BC Hydro and had suffered a major electrical shock on the job. I think he had steel plates in his forearm and elsewhere as a result. And what Alf discovered, to our delight, was that this somehow gave him seemingly superhuman powers. He could bend a quarter between his thumb and forefinger. He could tear a bottle cap in half with his fingers. This wasn't Penn and Teller sleight-of-hand stuff. We saw it with our own eyes many times. He could actually do it.

The Hydro accident also left Alf with the ability to resist electrocution. He'd carry with him an extension cord, which had been cut at the end to expose two bare wires. He'd plug it in and grab hold of the leads with no apparent effect. Then he'd tell us to form a chain by holding each other's forearms, and the two guys at the end would grab onto him. Sounds crazy, doesn't it? Who'd be stupid enough to do that? Us.

At first there was no effect. Then Alf would say, "Hang on tight boys, I'm letting a little juice through." And sure enough, you'd feel the current. Not a jolt, but an ever-increasing electrical flow that he'd let get stronger and stronger until someone finally cried uncle.

"Stop, Alf, stop!" One of us would yell, usually giving in pretty quickly.

Alf did other stuff too. He would put a light bulb in his mouth and illuminate it by grabbing the wires again. He'd do the old "wire in a pickle trick," holding it. And he would invite you to jump on his throat. This is where I drew the line. I watched but didn't take part. But it had no apparent effect on him, nor did a truck driving over his forearm, which was another of his favourites.

In fact, it was a video of that stunt, shot by friend and co-worker Kirk Duncan (with whom I worked for many years in

Victoria as well), that won Alf a spot on the 1980s TV show *That's Incredible*. If you're old enough, you'll remember it, one of the first-ever reality shows, hosted by John Davidson, Fran Tarkenton and Cathy Lee Crosby. (Years later, I golfed with her in a foursome that also included Tony Parsons and Arthur Griffiths, at the celebrity Pro-Am for the Air Canada Championship golf tournament.)

But Alf's taste of fame on TV didn't bring him riches. He'd been taken under the wing of another CKPG employee, Lorne Teachout, president of the union local, who took on the role of Alf's manager, but we'd still find Alf hanging out in the pub at night, ripping beer caps, bending quarters and entreating a table for a pint, so we assumed they never made any money.

These radio days might seem like prehistoric times for people who have grown up in the internet age, but radio offered a diversity of media services to local clients. For instance, CKPG supplied Muzak-style background music for local businesses. It came from big sixteen-inch open-reel tapes that played back slowly on a machine in the basement of the station, and played out via a phone line link.

An operator would switch the tapes, and we had a fairly big library of them. One day, for fun, someone took one of the reels, and about halfway to the end of the tape, spliced a recording of the Pink Floyd song, "Careful with that Axe, Eugene." If you are not familiar with the song, allow me to describe it. It starts low and slow, and sounds like it could be elevator music. Then it breaks into a sustained blood-curdling scream. It really isn't pleasant, and you could argue it really isn't music.

Out of the blue one day, the phone at the station began ringing off the hook—hotels and stores, doctors' and dentists' offices, all reporting the horrific screaming that was echoing through their establishments. There was an investigation worthy of Captain Queeg, whose strawberries went missing in *The Caine*

*Mutiny*. They never did determine who had played the trick. My co-worker, Terry Mather, the station engineer and an inveterate prankster, claims he had nothing to do with it.

Terry became a fast friend and a very good one. We had an obscene nickname for each other, the same name the angry logger called me at the Columbus. It somehow morphed into a falsetto vibrato when we addressed one another.

Within months of my move to Prince George in 1982, Terry and I became roommates, renting the home of Peter Clemente, the CKPG news director who had hired me. Mike Woodworth had assumed leadership of the newsroom shortly after I got there, and Peter left to join CKVU TV in Vancouver.

Though we were not model tenants, Terry and I did take care of the place and made sure the rent was paid. We did party a lot, but it was the '80s, and there wasn't much else to do. That house will also stand out in my mind for the "Cake Room," a bedroom so named for the shag carpet on the floor. The colours—pink, blue, yellow, white—made it look like a child's birthday cake. It was also our record library. Between the two of us, we probably had about six thousand lps. I would foolishly sell most of my vinyl later in Victoria.

Terry kept a machete in his closet, with which we disembowelled an effigy of New York Islanders' goalie Billy Smith on the front lawn, during the Stanley Cup playoffs one year. The neighbourhood children were delighted, their parents less so. He also had a waterbed, still a novelty at the time, in the basement. And he enjoyed hosting sleepovers in what came to be known as "Water World." No further information required.

We later rented another house that truly was a "water world." It was owned by a Prince George lawyer who was a partner in a local firm with Jack Heinrich, a Social Credit cabinet minister of the day. The house became known as the "Jacuzzi House." This split level was on a residential crescent just off Highway 16, near the intersection of Highway 97, where the local mascot, Mr. PG, a giant log-and-stick man made of fibreglass, stands sentinel. (To officially commemorate his birthday, CKPG put an aircheck, a recording of a newscast, into a time capsule that was sealed into his torso. I don't know when it gets opened. I hope in the future they can find a VHS machine, if they even know what that is.)

The Jacuzzi House looked a little like *The Brady Bunch* house from the outside, only we had more snow. What was remarkable about the house was the Jacuzzi for which it became known. In the cedar-lined rumpus room was the biggest hot tub you will likely ever see, running the entire width of the room, measuring about eight by sixteen feet. It was ridiculously big. Built into the basement window was a huge one-and-a-half horsepower fan connected to a humidistat. It would kick on automatically to exhaust the heat and steam. If we had been known for entertaining at Peter Clemente's house, we were entering a whole new world here, with a rec room to rival Hugh Hefner's Grotto.

Many a morning (or usually afternoon) we would awake to find the remnants of the night before. A layer of pink foam floating on the water, the shade of pink determined by how much makeup our guests had been wearing the night before. Floating plastic cups. Sometimes cigarette butts. It wasn't pretty. But a skimmer and a few cups full of granulated chlorine would do the trick, making it look like new again, ready for the following night's action.

There was a double door system at the entrance to the rumpus room, at the foot of the stairs in the entrance of the split-level home. The doors were there partly to muffle the noise of the fan, but mainly to block the vacuum effect when the exhaust fan came on. Unfortunately, the doors didn't always stay latched shut.

One evening, we were enjoying a blazing fire in the living room fireplace. We were negligent tenants, I suppose, in not having purchased a screen for the fireplace. The humidity downstairs hit the threshold. The fan switched on. The doors were sucked wide open. The fan was like a giant vacuum cleaner, finding a source of air wherever it could, which on this night was the chimney. It looked like something out of a cartoon. Before our bleary eyes, the burning logs literally jumped out of the fireplace and onto the living room floor. We got as many burns on our hands as there were in the carpet, returning the fiery logs and embers onto the fireplace grate. We never did get back our damage deposit.

The Jacuzzi House was a favourite hangout on Sundays, as buddies would gather for a day of football on TV. Inevitably, we would have failed to plan ahead and hoard some of our Saturday night beer for Sunday afternoon NFL consumption. Remember, this was circa 1984, and that meant that BC's liquor laws were not yet relaxed, as they would be a couple of years later for Expo 86. There were no beer and wine stores, and pubs were closed, so a restaurant was our only option. And we found a good one. There was a little eatery by the name of Casey's Steak Pit, located near the CN Rail yard as you head out of town eastbound on the Yellowhead Highway. It was run by a lovely woman called Mrs. Chow. I don't think we even knew her first name. I'm not sure we ever asked.

We would visit Mrs. Chow weekly for an early lunch, late on a Sunday morning. Usually we would order fries and gravy and a case of beer each, unopened. There was always a generous tip from us and a wink from Mrs. Chow, as we took home our "leftovers."

And we didn't just fill up on the NFL on those Sundays. By late in the afternoon, we'd pile into taxis, unless someone was the designated driver, and go back downtown to the Holiday Inn. It had the only TV sports bar in town (they were still a relatively new concept). The Holiday Inn had an all-you-can eat southern-fried chicken buffet every Sunday. Despite my years of eating KFC on the job in Salmon Arm, I still loved chicken (and still do). And we got our fill.

One week, one of us came up with the bright idea of bringing big plastic bags, which we would tuck into our parkas. After we consumed several platefuls on-site, we'd go back to the buffet one last time for a big final load of fried chicken, which would then ride home steaming in the bags inside our coats. We considered these leftovers, too. I'm sure they must have known. Our winter coats smelled like fried chicken all week.

Prince George was going through tough economic times when I was there. The first imposition of a softwood lumber tariff happened in 1982, and it hurt people who relied on the forest industry, which was just about everyone. And this was also the era of 23 percent mortgage rates. I knew a few people who walked away from their homes, handing the keys back to the bank. One of them was a friend who was storing my old Mustang in his carport after I had moved to Victoria. We hadn't been in a hurry for me to come back and get it, until he called one day to warn me he was about to default on his mortgage.

We got the car back in time. Patty's brother, Barry, his then-roommate and I made a fast trip to PG in Barry's truck with a U-Haul trailer to drag it back to Victoria. Unfortunately, the Code of The Road precludes me from going into any detail about the trip. I will tell you this much: the headlights on Barry's pickup shorted out en route and we drove from just north of Williams Lake to Prince George, about 225 kilometres, in the dark, with no lights. I'm not proud.

It wasn't all fun and games and parties in Prince George. We had a solid newsroom, and Mike Woodworth was a good leader. And though we were not far apart in age, he was a good mentor to me. I came away from CKPG a better newsman than the one who arrived after that long drive. I learned a lot. I am so glad to have spent time there, though I've only been back a couple of times and don't really stay in touch with anyone there anymore.

Had I known what a great experience Prince George would be, I would never have tried to get my old job back in Kamloops. I was disappointed and disillusioned when I got to PG (sorry, City of Prince George, no disrespect intended). I really wondered what

I had done. And I gave it a chance—at least a week or so, anyway. At that point I picked up the phone and called Doug Collins, my old news director at CFJC in Kamloops.

"Is it too late to change my mind? I'd like to come back," I implored.

Doug's advice was to stick it out. And in retrospect, he was right. You can't go back, even if you do go with your tail between your legs. I would learn later that the Prince George job offer might not have come out of the blue. I'm told Peter Clemente called CFJC to see if there was anyone they knew looking for work.

"Yes," he was apparently told, "Hudson Mack."

That came as a bit of a shock, but maybe it shouldn't have. The CFJC staff had become very polarized in the midst of a negative workplace environment. It was a unionized operation, a closed shop represented by the National Association of Broadcast Employees and Technicians (NABET), which eventually got swallowed up by the Communications, Energy and Paperworkers, and is now under the Unifor umbrella. The union local leadership didn't like the management. And the company, co-owned by the two managers, really didn't like the union.

This was my first job in the business, so I was new to all of this.

I had done my workplace practicum at CFJC in the spring of 1980. As unpaid internships go, this was a good one. Kamloops is only about an hour's drive from Salmon Arm, where my mom and sister, and many of my friends, still lived. And CFJC, unlike many other stations, was willing to put students on the air if they were capable. Doug was a good news director, a big man whose nickname was "Brahma," presumably from his coverage and calling of the rodeos in the area.

I was put on the air immediately, writing and delivering a fifteen-minute newscast at 9:30 each morning. I'm not sure exactly who was watching. The newscast was sandwiched between the Christian daytime talk show *100 Huntley Street* and children's program *The Friendly Giant*. It was good experience, though. And I was able to report for radio as well as TV. One of the friends I made at CFJC that spring was John Pollard, who ran promotions, and whose father was a manager and co-owner of the station. Our paths would cross again later in Victoria. John was the GM who orchestrated the 2009 employee purchase of CHEK TV when it was abandoned by Canwest.

Unfortunately, when the month was up, so was I. Doug and the others seemed to like me, but there were no jobs. So I returned to Salmon Arm for the summer and got my old job back at the government liquor store. As another long, hot Salmon Arm summer was drawing to a close in late August, I was beginning to worry. I had tapes and resumes out all over the place, and finally, one afternoon, the phone rang.

On the line was a man named Mike Goetz, news director at CFCW radio in Camrose, Alberta, southeast of Edmonton. He explained that he'd received my name from one of my instructors at SAIT, CFCN anchor Darrel Janz. He told me I was highly recommended and that he'd like a tape ASAP, and that it was probably academic, because based on what he'd heard, he was ready to hire me now. I still don't quite understand what happened next, except that, as a fatalist, I can only assume my career and life was not intended to go in that direction.

"Well, thank you, Mr. Goetz," I began. "I am flattered at your offer and appreciate it very much. But I think I'd like to stay in BC and work in television, if I can."

A brief pause. "I see. Well, thank you for your time. Goodbye."

I looked at the phone, wondering if I had rocks in my head, as my mom used to say. I later learned that CFCW radio was a big station, even if it was in a small town. It was the fifty-thousand-watt voice of agricultural central Alberta. And it probably was a squandered opportunity for someone starting out. I also found out more about the late Mike Goetz, who died in 1995, and how highly respected he was in the industry.

I had a pit in my stomach like one I would feel about five years later, but the outcome this time was eerily similar to then. As I stewed about slamming the door on opportunity knocking, the phone rang again in a few days. It was "Brahma" calling from Kamloops.

"Would you like to come back to CFJC, and get paid this time?" Doug Collins asked.

I didn't even ask about money. I was in. The previous news anchor had been dismissed after appearing to be drunk on the air one night. I jumped at the chance. I worked with, and learned from, some great people in Kamloops. The newsroom was strong. Doug was a good newsman and a kind teacher.

Anchor and reporter Stu Blakely was another early mentor in Kamloops. He was a former Mountie with a taste for hand-guns and rum-and-coke. Stu was a great newsman with a flawless delivery, known for signing off his newscasts with "Remember, we'd rather be talking at you, not about you." He left the business in 1996, and died a few years ago.

One night Stu dragged me through a cloud of cyanide. Really. A transport truck carrying cyanide pellets had crashed coming down the Columbia Street hill in Kamloops, flipping and spilling its toxic load at the entrance to Royal Inland Hospital. Our cameraman wasn't answering his pager, and I was still fresh enough out of school to remember how to shoot. So Stu called me out and I was his cameraman. As he led me behind the yellow tape at the scene, Mounties yelled at him to get out, as rain started to fall on the pellets, triggering the chemical reaction that released the poison gas. In the end, I was all right and so was Stu, as well as the hundreds of patients standing by to evacuate the hospital. But I learned something that night, about Stu and about myself.

Another legendary example of Stu's tenacity was when he reportedly threatened to break the arm of a CBC national reporter travelling with Prime Minister Trudeau. There was a whis-tle-stop news conference on the airport tarmac during an election campaign. The Ottawa press gallery was there covering the PM, and when, for the third time, the CBC's Bill Casey moved Stu's microphone and its big CFJC News mic flasher, my friend made it clear that if the mic moved again, Mr. Casey's wrist would go with it. The mic stayed put.

It was a good time to be starting out. But there was a negative vibe in the building, too, as the union and the company made life miserable for each other. The station hired a former Steelworkers union leader from the nearby copper mine to act as "industrial relations manager"—unnecessary, I think, for a staff this size.

There was weird stuff. On payday, you had to visit the accountant's office and stand at his desk while he thumbed through the paycheques and looked disdainfully at yours before glancing up, then handing it over like a bowl of gruel in *Oliver Twist*.

"Please, sir, I want some more."

He once told me I was lucky they left the photocopier turned on and unlocked in the evening. I used it to copy radio scripts for the TV production crew on the late news. I didn't really think I was being done any special favours.

I was neither pro- nor anti-union. But I was put off when I learned that after courting me for support and membership, the NABET local was fighting to get back the job of the anchor I had replaced, which would have put me out the door.

The final straw, for me, may have come on the day of the station's twenty-fifth anniversary. We had a special retrospective report prepared for the newscast that night. And there was a reception at the studio for invited guests. The union thought this would be a good day for an informational picket line. Anyone in the bargaining unit, and that was everyone except management, was expected to stay out. Like any picket line in a union shop, you crossed at your peril. I thought it was outrageous and let it be known, but I didn't cross. And, there I was, reluctantly, in the photos of picketers that the industrial relations officer was taking from his office window.

So, in this emotionally charged workplace, I had fallen out of favour with both sides. The union thought I was on the company side, and management saw me as part of the union. Two years into my first job in the business, I didn't think it would go like this.

I knew I was ready for a change. And that's when Peter Clemente called from CKPG.

I had the same feeling nearly three years later in Prince George, when once again opportunity came knocking. I was approached by Dennis McVarish, who was the Executive Producer at CBC Edmonton. They knew of me and wanted a tape, which I provided. He flew me in for a weekend, I read an audition and had an interview. It was only part-time to start, three days a week, reporting on Friday and anchoring on the weekend. There was no promise, but before long it would likely be full-time, and from there, who knows?

The meeting went well. I think the audition read did too, and Dennis seemed to like me. He called after I got home to Prince George and offered me the job. Now I faced a dilemma. I was ready to move, and this was a great opportunity. But it was Edmonton. And as dumb as that may sound, it's what kept me from accepting the offer.

I don't know if there is mind control exercised on newborns, subliminal audiotapes played in the nurseries at maternity hospitals in Calgary and Edmonton, but these two cities just don't like each other, at least they didn't then. I was only five years removed from having lived in Calgary, and still considered myself a native Calgarian, and I just couldn't see moving to Edmonton and being loyal to the place. There really wasn't a more logical explanation than that.

"I'm sorry," I told Dennis, "I just don't have an affinity for Edmonton, and I think to do a good job for you, I need to feel that. I'm afraid I have to decline your offer with thanks."

Pause. "Okay," he said, "give it some more thought, and I will call you back in a week."

When the phone rang the next time, my mind was unchanged.

"If you are sure," he said, "I accept your decision, even if I don't agree. Make sure this is what you want, because I'm not going to call again."

"Thanks very much," I said, hanging up the phone.

I might not have known better that summer in Salmon Arm, when I was offered a job in Camrose that I didn't really want, straight out of school. But I should have had more sense this time. And I should have said yes, I kept telling myself. The voice in my head was screaming at me. I blew it. An opportunity to join the CBC in a bigger market, who knows where that might have led. I descended into a great funk, until I found out where it led a few weeks later, when CHEK TV called.

# 8

## CHEK TV

Imagine getting out of jail. Or think back, and remember what it was like. Joking aside, this is a fairly apt analogy for my coming to Victoria from Prince George. (Again, please don't take offence, City of Prince George.)

I do not mean it as an insult, though on my first night on the air in Victoria, during banter with sportscaster Robin Adair, I opined, "The best thing about Prince George is Highway 97 south." I was being glib and a bit of a smartass, and we weren't on a satellite at the time, so no one there would see it, right? (Interestingly, Robin had had a hand in my move to Victoria. He'd seen me on a visit to his ex-wife in Prince George, and when CHEK needed a new late anchor, he mentioned me to the news director.) Well, as it turned out, someone did see it. Monica Becott, who was a Prince George city councillor and a friend, happened to be in Victoria that night, on business with the Provincial Capital Commission. There she was, in her hotel, watching my Victoria debut, excited at the opportunity. She had even given me a parting gift on behalf of her and my other friends at PG city hall. And what do I say about the city? Nothing good. She mailed me a note later to say how disappointed she was, and how hurtful she found the comment. I learned a lesson that night. At least, I hope so.

But when I say prison, I mean only that arriving in Victoria at the beginning of April was literally a breath of fresh air. In Prince George, I left behind a long, dark, cold winter. Spring was in the air in Prince George as well, but the two-storey mounds of dirty snow plowed into the corners of shopping mall parking lots had to melt first, and when they did, a winter's worth of litter, gravel and salt would be left behind. Lawns would be brown, and trees would be budless for several weeks more.

When I arrived in Victoria, the blossoms had come and gone and the trees were already leafy. Everything was so green. The fragrance of flowers was in the air, like in Hawaii. Manicured yards and gardens were already well into their growing season. And it was warm. It could not have been more beautiful, or more different.

There was something freeing about being here, too. The getting-out-of-prison analogy is a reflection of the isolation you feel when you live in the north. Prince George is the hub for the central and northern part of the province, but it is many hours away from a larger metropolitan area, and in 1985 did not have many of the amenities it does today, nor the sense of global connection the internet has given us. I enjoyed living there, and I wish I hadn't offended with my little "joke" on my first Victoria newscast.

When I joined CHEK TV in 1985, I assumed it would put me on a career track that would keep me in one place for a couple of years or maybe a few, and then I'd move again, onward and upward. But living on Vancouver Island is a hard habit to break.

When I came to CHEK, I produced and anchored the late news, and within a couple of years, I had moved up to the evening news at 5:30 and had been named Assistant News Director. The change happened sooner than I might have expected, after anchor and Assistant ND Mark Jam Vrem left the station to become the News Director at ITV in Edmonton.

We were very successful at CHEK. The ratings were good, and although at the time we were the only game in town for TV news, we still competed in the Greater Vancouver market. Television news in Victoria is unique in Canada, in that it is a relatively small, central market, competing against much larger stations and newsrooms in a nearby much larger market (Vancouver). And there is also tremendous penetration by the stations from Seattle. So viewers expect a lot. You're a player in the second-most lucrative English language market in Canada, and holding your own against stations in the number twelve market in the US.

At the time, CHEK was owned by Western International Communications (WIC), the company owned by Vancouver's Griffiths family, which launched a media empire that grew from the purchase of radio titan CKNW, the "top dog." The WIC stable of stations stretched across western Canada, and the jewel in the crown was the eight-hundred-pound gorilla of local news, BCTV. We benefited from strong leadership, led by a general manager for whom I had and have enormous respect: Roy Gardner. He is now retired in the Okanagan, but he recently stepped back in to help CHEK during its uncertain times with employee ownership.

Roy would eventually leave for BCTV, with whom we were still affiliated. Jim Nicholl became GM, which led to the eventual and not unexpected demise of CHEK news director Tony Cox, who had hired me from Prince George a few years earlier after I spurned the Edmonton offer. Tony had also made a play for the GM's job and was passed over, and it was well known within the station that he and Jim were often at odds.

So, it fell to me to lead the newsroom on a caretaker basis while the search began for a replacement for Tony. I put my hand up but was passed over for Rick Wiertz, who had been covering the legislature for Vancouver station CKVU, which was then known as U.TV. I was not entirely surprised not to get the job, but thought

I was ready for it, even though I didn't really want to go off the air. It may have been difficult to do both, because as an on-air employee, I was mandated to be a member of the union, in what was known as a closed shop.

Rick was a good newsman and did a good job. He was loyal to me and supported me even when it appeared there was a move afoot to replace me on the evening news by an ambitious reporter who had begun chumming around with the GM, water-skiing on Shawnigan Lake and, I suspected, plotting my overthrow. Rick stuck with me, perhaps at his own peril.

Rick was an interesting guy. I'm big on nicknames, and for some reason he became "The Bhagwan." I guess it was around the time of the Oregon-based spiritual guru Bhagwan Shree Rajneesh's rise to prominence. They didn't really have much in common other than that they both had beards and both collected vintage cars, and, as assignment editor Dave Biro and I agreed, they both exercised mind control.

Rick was also what technology buffs would call an "early adopter." He was really into computers and was the first person to show me the internet. Computerization of our newsroom had just happened a year or so before he got there, dumb terminals linked to a mainframe. And I was initially tasked with running the backup tapes each week. Sometimes I forgot. Before long there'd be PCs on every desk and someone in charge of IT. But back then, it was magic wand stuff, and Rick was the sorcerer. In fact he sold me our first home computers, and later, when he left broadcasting, he ran a leading computer and technology store (before the internet put that out of business).

Rick was also known for not being around in the newsroom too much. Sometimes we didn't know where he was, although he did assure us in a news meeting one day, "If I'm not here, I'm somewhere." And we could reach him on the new technology of cellphones, the big square brick models. Back then, the newsroom only had a couple that floated around.

During this period, I had become involved in what was then known as the Radio-Television News Directors Association (RTNDA) and was the convention chair of the national RTNDA Canada conference in Victoria in 1994, which was a big job. Usually, there is an on-site committee, but in a city with relatively few stations and people, there wasn't a large pool to draw from. The convention went well, and there was a move to nominate me for president that year. Out of the blue, at least to me, Rick decided he wanted to do it, and he was elected. I was still on the board of directors as VP of television, and as it turned out, health issues kept Rick from travelling that year, so I attended the regional conferences across Canada on his behalf as de facto president.

The disappearing act may have caught up with Rick, because a couple of years later, he parted company with the station, and GM Jim Nicholl was on the prowl for a new ND. Again, I applied, this time more confident that with more experience, and a willingness to go off the air if necessary, I might stand a better chance. I also got the sense that the union might be willing to negotiate an appendix to the contract, allowing me to at least read the newscast, if not work on it, as a manager.

It all happened again around the national RTNDA convention, my first as president. It was 1995, the first year the association had teamed up with the Canadian Association of Broadcasters (CAB) to hold a joint conference, in Edmonton. There was a large contingent of station managers and executives from WIC at the convention, since they always went to the CAB. Also, it was my first year to choose, as president, that year's recipient of the RTNDA President's Award. I selected my friend and colleague, BCTV anchor Tony Parsons.

But the subplot at the convention was Jim Nicholl's news director search. I had scheduled a job interview with him on our return to Victoria, and I hoped that my stock would rise after he had seen the RTNDA and me in action, especially my decision to honour Tony, the company's biggest star. But in a conversation after the awards dinner, Robert Palmer, who was then news director at WIC's Red Deer station, RDTV, told me he was having breakfast in the morning to finalize details of his move to Victoria. Jim had hired him as my newest news director. I wasn't bitter, and Robert was and is a good friend, but I was disappointed and felt betrayed. (If you're keeping track, this is now the second time I've been passed over to become news director at CHEK. Don't put your score pad away.)

The Robert Palmer era at CHEK News only lasted a couple of years, and they were tumultuous ones, though not of his making. The ground was shifting under the station, with new ownership in the offing. WIC CEO and patriarch Frank Griffiths died in 1994, and leadership of the corporation fell to his sons. The business landscape is littered with family-owned companies that struggle once the second generation takes over. I will leave it to the MBAS to decide if that's what happened here, but it wasn't long before Izzy Asper and Global had purchased the TV properties. In the lead-up to the sale, the station was cutting spending and staff. It was around this time that Patty was able to negotiate a buyout, but she didn't think Robert made it easy for her.

Leading the cutbacks was the recently appointed GM who had replaced Jim Nicholl. His name was Warren Olson and he was the former comptroller at BCTV. This was the era when we complained that the accountants were wrecking broadcasting. A slender man, Warren earned the nickname "The Slim Reaper," but eventually he downsized himself out of a job too, after he had finished making sufficient cuts to staff.

We had a much less sinister nickname for Robert Palmer: Pee Wee. It wasn't intended to belittle him. He simply bore a vague resemblance to TV's Pee Wee Herman, who still had a following in those days. But if the CHEK newsroom was "Pee Wee's Playhouse," the party didn't last long, as management changed again. Robert

Palmer was soon gone—though by his own hand. There is something about people from Alberta. They can tolerate forty-below temperatures, as long as the sun is shining, as it usually is on those cold Calgary days. But tolerating rainy West Coast winters is a different kind of challenge. And so it was for Robert's wife, who never adjusted to the endless stretch of wet and grey, though mild, days that define winter on the BC coast. She wanted to move back to Calgary, so Robert left. He stayed in television news when he got there, working under the legendary Del Archer at CFCN. (Del, by the way, is one of the nicest guys you'll ever meet.) As a native Calgarian myself, I liked the change in the weather, though it is just one of the things that has kept me on Vancouver Island.

As assistant news director, it was my responsibility, again, to keep the trains running on time, and so I did, as I launched my latest gambit to be promoted to the news director's office. Our new GM was Craig Roskin, who had been sales manager at WIC's ITV in Edmonton. Craig was a breath of fresh air, a genuinely nice guy and a smart manager. His style and approach with staff lifted a cloud off the station. The ND hire wasn't his to make alone, though. The regional VP of news at BCTV was Steve Wyatt. And he didn't like the concept of news director as anchor or vice versa. Much of his opposition, I think, was based on the less than exceptional outcome at BCTV, when Tony Parsons had been made ND and stayed on the air. That experiment didn't last long, and by many accounts didn't go well. Although Tony had a tough row to hoe, presiding over the news operation and making staff cutbacks, and then dealing with an especially bitter strike.

The writing was on the wall. Wyatt wasn't buying. And before long, I found out why. A rising star at BCTV was coming to CHEK. Veteran newspaperman Ian Haysom had recently wiped the ink off his hands at the *Vancouver Sun* and joined BCTV on their assignment desk. Ian is a smart guy and a good newsman, and if you have enough time, he'll tell you all about it. (Ian, I'm only joking.) What he, at first, didn't know about TV was more than offset by his keen news sense and experience, which stretched back to Fleet Street in London. Growing up in that cutthroat tabloid world had sharpened Ian's chops. He was fiercely competitive. If you couldn't beat the other guy on a story, then you could certainly find a way to spoil it. Ian's years in the Vancouver print media, and the time he spent in the BCTV newsroom under ND Keith Bradbury's tutelage, made him a good choice to lead a TV news department of his own.

Do you see a pattern emerging here? Mark your scorecard. I've now been passed over for the job a third time.

Please let me digress for a moment about the late Keith Bradbury. Though I never worked for him directly, I have the world of respect for him. He and Cameron Bell revolutionized television news, and not just in Vancouver, when they built BCTV into a journalistic juggernaut. By extension, they revolutionized the industry, as other stations emulated what was going on in that Burnaby newsroom. I don't really know Cameron, and I didn't know Keith well. But I sure admired him. He was tough, unrelenting and quietly intimidating.

Back to CHEK. Ian arrived, the purse strings loosened and we started hiring again. Show producers were hired so the anchors wouldn't have to perform both roles. A bright up-and-comer from BCTV joined the staff. Rob Germain, who had been producer of their noon news, came to CHEK as assignment editor. The station also invested in new technology, though some of it was what we called "CHAN-Me-Downs," cast-offs from BCTV (whose actual call letters are CHAN). And CHEK, now running leaner and more efficiently, began firing on all cylinders.

It was around this time that consultancy was in full flight in TV newsrooms. And we were not immune. The practice was widespread in the US and was growing in Canada. Consulting companies, such as Frank N. Magid and Associates, and Audience Research and Development (AR&D), were making inroads in this country, after becoming ubiquitous in the US. We had a contract under Global with AR&D. The Texas-based company sent one of their best, Mark Toney, to Victoria to analyze our operation and on-air product. He put on some good workshops, and I got something out of it, even if it didn't bring an overhaul of the newscast.

I like consultants. One of the brightest in the industry is a good friend, Graeme Newell of 602 Communications. And I have always liked what Mackie Morris has to say about writing and good storytelling. Critics decry consultants' influence on local news, and it's true that for a long time, local newscasts across the US, and everywhere, all looked pretty much the same (and, to a certain extent, still do). It's also true in Canada, but to a lesser extent. And the interesting thing about Canadians is we always seem to think the Americans know better, whether we admit it to ourselves or not. A homegrown consultant might offer input that's just as valid and valuable, but one of our own couldn't know more than us, could they?

In addition to the input of the outside consultants, we were also seeking the wisdom of in-house news guru Keith Bradbury, in semi-retirement from BCTV. We were getting ready for head-to-head competition at last. There had been a clamour for a second television licence to serve Vancouver Island. Finally, in the late 1990s, the broadcast regulator, the CRTC, issued a call for applications for the new licence and scheduled hearings. Whatever was coming was still quite a ways off, but we would no longer have the playground all to ourselves.

The eventual arrival of a new competitor on the island coincided with a seismic shift in the media landscape in the Vancouver extended market over 2000 and 2001. It was musical chairs in affiliation and ownership.

(Try to stay with me here. There will be a test. No, no test.)

Ontario-based Baton Broadcasting, which was the backbone of the CTV network, launched a new station in Vancouver called VTV (CIVT). The writing was on the wall that the CTV programming and affiliation in British Columbia would soon leave BCTV and CHEK. The CanWest Global purchase of those two stations was approved by the CRTC, which meant Global had to divest itself of its existing Vancouver station, CKVU. It was sold to Toronto-based CHUM, known for its edgy attitude, walking-talking, rock and roll CityPulse news format, and the occasional blue movie. It was still run at the time by self-styled media visionary Moses Znaimer.

The ironic thing for CHUM was that it didn't have a presence in BC before that sale. And it had just won the licence sweepstakes for the new Victoria station, which was now in the works. It didn't really want a station in Victoria, but there was nothing available in Vancouver at the time. Now it would have two stations in the market, not necessarily a bad thing. The duopoly, as it was known, of CHAN and CHEK was something that had been grandfathered to WIC and was jealously guarded. The opportunity for one company to sell advertising on two signals in the same market had dollar signs written all over it. At least, that was true then, when there were still dollar signs written on conventional television in Canada.

The CanWest Global ownership came at a time of tremendous expansion and growth for the Winnipeg-based company in broadcast and print. The company was on a buying spree, snatching up broadcast properties and newspapers. It launched a second national paper, the *National Post*, to take on *The Globe and Mail*. The over-reach would be its eventual demise following the death of patriarch Izzy Asper. (Remember what we were saying earlier about what happens when the kids take over an established family business empire?)

The CanWest era brought us "convergence," though the marriage of CanWest broadcast and print operations would bring mixed results. It felt funny at first. We were still the only TV station in Victoria, for a little while yet, and our de facto local competition had always been the *Times Colonist* newspaper. So it was anathema to us, sharing stories and leads with each other, now that CHEK and the TC were both under the CanWest banner. They thought it was weird at the TC too.

The best convergence example of "never the twain shall meet" came when we did a joint investigation with the TC. I forget what the story was, but we were each doing companion pieces, and we wanted to get their print reporters on the air. Most of them hated it. Few would even do it, and for those who did, there was always a lot of hyperventilating first. I always used to think that broadcast people wanted to see their name in a byline in print, and paper people wanted to see themselves on TV. Now I'm not so sure.

One day, TC reporter Denise Helm came to the station to rehearse and record a studio standup for her piece. I don't think we had planned to do it live; we knew they weren't ready for that. Producer Richard Konwick and I were in the studio with her. Denise was a pro, but she was terribly nervous, reading and rereading her script. Agonizing over what she was going to say and if it sounded right. All the while, Richard and I were concerning ourselves over where she should stand, where the lighting would be most flattering, which shot made the set look good. A moment like this perhaps exemplifies why some print people have always considered broadcast journalists to be the superficial, bastard cousins in the Capital-J journalism family.

Convergence never really panned out and wouldn't until news on the internet forced everyone onto the same playing field. Now the "silos" (to use a hackneyed phrase) have been torn down. We are content providers regardless of the platform.

In the midst of this mix, the vacancy sign went back up outside the newsroom corner office at CHEK. Ian Haysom had served his apprenticeship as a news director, and Global was ready to move him back to Vancouver to take over the BCTV/Global news machine.

The Vancouver station adopted the hybrid branding for a long time after the ownership change, believing the BCTV brand was too potent to give up. I think they overestimated its staying power, and they finally dropped it for, simply, Global. They may have been motivated by CTV, which was now the outright owner of VTV, which rebranded it BC CTV to try to mess with BCTV News on Global and create confusion. Is it any wonder viewers often don't really know who they're watching?

When Ian went back to Vancouver, I told him that I thought this was going to be my opportunity. The timing was right. I had more experience, and the recent reorganization introducing show producers would make it possible for me to present the newscast each night, in addition to my news director duties. Dispensation from the union might have allowed me to read it on air, but not to undertake the writing or production of it ahead of time, since that would be bargaining unit work. Turns out that was an agreement with the union we wouldn't have to negotiate.

Ian assured me that I had his support, and that he would go to bat for me in the application and interview process. After all, we had worked well together and he knew what I could do. I felt confident that this was my time. But something changed. Out of the blue, one day, Rob Germain told me Ian had encouraged him to put his hand up for the job, and that he would support him to try to make it happen. What happened? I think that once again, Steve Wyatt's trepidation about a news director on the air overrode any willingness to take a chance on it. Maybe that's what Ian discovered when he got back to Burnaby, and that's why he changed horses in midstream. Maybe they just didn't want me to do it, or didn't think I could. I don't know and it doesn't matter now.

But, just for the sake of it, I hope you have been keeping track. This was now the fourth time I had been passed over for the news director's job at CHEK. You only have to hit me over the head so many times before the message starts sinking in.

Rob and I had a good working relationship and are still friends. He's a good news director, but I wonder sometimes if this was really the job he wanted. He was an outstanding assignment editor and as news director sometimes didn't really seem to want to give that up. My attitude did not suffer, but I would be a liar if I tried to tell you that I wasn't disappointed and increasingly disillusioned.

I had turned forty, I had been at CHEK more than fifteen years at the time, and I sensed I might be approaching something of a crossroads, though I never gave that sort of thing much thought. I loved the news business, but I also loved Victoria. The new CHUM station, which would be branded The New VI when it was scheduled to sign on in the fall of 2001, showed no interest in me. And that didn't surprise me. They had raided a few of our people, mostly news photographers and production staff, but on the air, they wanted to be new and different, the Anti-CHEK. I didn't fit into that plan. Little did I know what the future would bring.

# 9
## My Mom

Whenever I talk about growing up and the big influences on my life, it usually involves my career and broadcasting, and because of that, by default I talk about my dad and my brother. But I should really give my mother's story the attention it deserves. Isn't that usually the way with unsung moms?

My mother was born Murdena Cathrine McGregor, on Christmas Eve 1918. I always thought she got a raw deal having her birthday on Christmas Eve. But it made gift giving easy. Her parents, as you'd guess with a name like that, were of Scottish descent, coming to Canada and settling in Calgary via Kinkardine, Ontario. Her father, Murdoch, was a carpenter who built many of the houses as Calgary grew in the early 1900s, including the home she was born in. Her mother, who had two other children, boys older and younger than my mom, was named Lachena. It is pronounced in that Scottish way, like you are trying to clear a fur ball from your throat. Both of them died before I was born.

My mother was forty-two when I was born in 1960, which was getting pretty old for bearing children at the time, though

I was her fourth child. That may be normal now but was less so then. And she nearly hemorrhaged to death after the delivery. She would later describe her near-death experience, floating over her hospital bed, watching frantic doctors and nurses below her as she nearly died.

It isn't just the Oedipus in me when I say that I thought my mom was beautiful. I always thought she looked a little like the Queen in her youth, which might explain my enduring affection for the monarch. She had jet-black hair, which she eventually let go grey gracefully, and a lovely complexion. She was one of the first I knew to keep her face out of the sun, though she and my dad loved travelling to where it was hot when Calgary was cold. She had a great sense of humour and loved a good laugh. She also suffered from hay fever and could be heard all around the old neighbourhood when she sneezed. The allergies were something I inherited. When I was a kid, we used to get shots for them, which I hated.

Murdene, as she was known to friends, was a nurse, and a great one. She was in the Class of 1941 from the Calgary General Hospital, and she would dutifully attend class reunions for many years. She worked for years in a downtown clinic, at the office of a prominent Calgary urologist.

When Leilani and I were little, she chose to stay at home. She'd be known today as a "stay-at-home mom." Then, it was known simply as "mom." (Thanks for that, Willie Geist!) There was something comforting about a hot lunch at home. I hated it in Calgary when it was too cold to walk home at lunch, and you'd have to eat in the gym, breathing in whatever it was the other kids had brought. Mostly tuna sandwiches and peanut butter. This was long before kids had food allergies and peanut butter was verboten.

We never really had a lot to do with my mom's relatives, though I did know them slightly better than the ones on my dad's side. He probably had something to do with the sporadic contact, because he wanted as little to do with her family as he did his own.

She had an older brother, Jack, who was about six foot six inches tall and rail-thin. He was an anesthetist in Regina.

We called my mom's younger brother, Byron, Uncle "Bud." He got that nickname from his mother when he suffered a childhood illness. "Oh, he's just a little bud," she reportedly said at the time. The name stuck. He got better from whatever it was, by the way. In any event, we didn't see much of them, aunts or uncles or cousins. Jack's youngest daughter, Marguerite, did turn up at my mom's funeral. It was good of her to come.

Bud had three kids, one of whom became an anti-war activist after her fiancé was killed in Vietnam. His son is a golf pro, which makes me think this is a connection I should try to restore. And Bud's other daughter lived in southern California. Patty and I visited her in Newport Beach in the 1980s, but I haven't been in touch since.

The fact is, I do not do a very good job of staying in touch with people. I haven't talked to my brother's widow in nearly a year, though there is no rift or anything to cause that. I just never pick up the phone. And during my mom's latter years in Calgary, especially when she moved in with my sister, I was not in very close touch. Does a son's guilt ever go away?

My mother was even more selfless than most, and that was never clearer than when my dad got sick. She had been out of nursing for decades but realized she needed to go back to work. So in 1973, at the age of fifty-five, she went back to nursing school. To recertify as a Registered Nurse, she had to take a refresher course, and the closest place she could do that was Kamloops, 120 kilometres away from Salmon Arm. Every weekday, for six months, she drove to and from Kamloops to attend the program at Royal Inland Hospital. And to make the task even more arduous, she encountered resistance and blatant ageism by her supervisor, who made her life miserable. All this with two teenagers at home and a husband being treated for cancer, facing an uncertain prognosis.

She got her RN again and went back to work, at the hospital in Salmon Arm, working shifts around the clock. I think work was a tonic for her. She loved her job and was a natural nurse. She especially loved drawing blood and was always noticing the veins on peoples' arms, taking great delight in the good-looking ones, imagining sticking in a needle. As anyone who has undergone a hospital stay knows, a nurse who can find a vein on the first try is worth her or his weight in gold.

After my dad died, she continued to work until she was forced to stop at the mandatory retirement age. She didn't really stop then, though. Later, after she moved back to Calgary, she worked for several more years, doing paramedical exams for insurance companies. She found many more good veins and kept hitting the ones that were hard to find.

My mother never remarried, because she said she didn't think it was fair to Leilani and me to have a new man in her life, at this stage in ours. I'm sure she was lonely at times, and there was no shortage of suitors, including a widowed doctor from the town of Chase, who was very fond of her.

Murdene was extremely wise, but with a childlike awe and enthusiasm. She was devoted to her children and family and took great pride in our successes, though she worried about my brother.

She travelled to China with a group of nurses, before tourism became normal in that country. And though she was never a braggart, for years she enjoyed working that China trip into the conversation whenever she could.

And she was loyal to her friends, most of whom she lost over the years.

She enjoyed good health into her old age but began to slow after breaking her hip. She had travelled to Mexico with my sister and her daughter and husband. They had just arrived at their resort when she tripped on a marble stair while arriving in the open-air lobby in Cancun. She had told me before they left that she thought it was outrageous how much she'd had to pay for out-of-country medical insurance, since this was her first trip outside of Canada since turning eighty.

It's a good thing she did. Because she was covered, she was flown back to Calgary in an air ambulance, to have hip replacement surgery at home and not in Mexico. The surgery was done at the hospital where, several years later, she would die of natural causes, peacefully in her sleep. She was eighty-seven. Pneumonia, "the old person's friend," she used to say. Only a nurse would know about that.

I think of my mother often. When people ask me about my heroes, and the people who shaped my life, I make sure I don't just talk about my dad and brother, who inspired me to get into broadcasting. I talk about my mom, who always put us first.

# 10

## Gary and Byron

I idolized my big brother. And for the most part, I did it from afar. He was twelve years older than me and he moved away from home when he was eighteen. He was kind, and maybe the most generous person I've ever known. No, there's no maybe about it.

Gary Lachlan Mack was a complicated guy. His middle name was a nod to my mom's Scottish roots. I think it was the name of a cousin of hers she'd had a crush on as a kid. And he embraced that Scots history in a big way, when he took MacGregor as his professional name on the radio. He was known in Windsor and Detroit, and throughout broadcasting and beyond, as Byron MacGregor. But he never legally changed his name, and we always knew him as Gary. I'll switch back and forth, referring to him as Gary and Byron. If the dual identity felt like multiple personalities to him, it did to us too. People in Windsor and Detroit, including his wife, Jo-Jo, knew him as Byron, of course. Family and friends in Calgary knew him as Gary. I would call him Gary in conversation, but Byron with people who knew him as that; often, when referring to him in the third person, I would opt for the more generic "my brother."

I think the dual identity may have troubled him, wondering who he really was. I know the horror of that December day in 1956, when he discovered Darrel in the garage, must have scarred him for life.

In the mid-1960s, he was in his element. He was the class president in his senior year at Western Canada High School. He was a star on the football team. He and buddies Thom Nelson and Glen Wright (longtime Calgary broadcaster known as Arnie Jackson) ran the school's information source, delivering a daily newscast called "The Voice of Western" over the PA every morning. And he was doing the real radio thing, covering overnight weekend DJ shifts at CFAC, hired by my dad when he was the program director at the station.

I was too young at the time to understand the roots of whatever rift there was between my brother and my dad. Rift might be the wrong word. But there was a strain in their relationship. It probably had something to do with his and Darrel's childhood. I think the Clarence who Leilani and I knew was a mellower dad than the one raising his first two kids. Maybe Gary subconsciously blamed my dad for what had happened.

One thing that I know did lead to hard feelings between Gary and my dad was football. The year he graduated from high school, Gary and another teammate from the Western Redmen football team were invited to a walk-on tryout for the CFL's Calgary Stampeders. My dad wouldn't sign the consent form. He wasn't into sports and thought football was brutal. The other player did eventually sign with the Stamps and went on to a CFL Hall of Fame career. His name is Rudy Linterman.

When I watch Sheldon (and earlier, Hamilton) on the football field, I can't help but think about my dad and Gary and football. Sometimes I think Sheldon looks like Gary at that age in his pads and helmet. Maybe it's my imagination. And I feel for Clarence, especially worrying about football injuries. I can understand Clarence's concern for his son's safety, with the loss of Darrel still just a few years in the past. But this led to a chill in their relationship. I also think there were issues at CFAC; it's not always easy working for your father, and not always easy being your son's boss.

So, in 1966, Gary left Calgary and moved to Winnipeg, where he launched his radio career as a DJ at CKRC. I don't know exactly what happened in Winnipeg and probably never will. But it didn't end well. I remember a hasty drive across the prairies, and moving him back to Calgary. From there he moved to Yorkton, Saskatchewan, and CJGX, and it was there that he moved into news. And this stint in his career is an example of what a small world broadcasting is. The station was co-owned by George Gallagher and Ed Laurence. Ed is the grandfather of Mira Laurence, with whom I worked for ten years in Victoria. And Gary's morning show partner was DJ Dan McAllister. Dan and I would briefly cross paths years later in Kamloops on opposing stations, and we then became good friends in Victoria, where he was longtime GM of The Q, the top rock station in town. Small world.

In 1967, Gary and Dan put a joint ad in *Broadcaster Magazine* under the heading "Your One-Two Punch in the Morning, We're Good!" Their hubris caught the attention of legendary news director Dick Smyth at CKLW in Windsor. He didn't want or need a morning DJ, but he did want a newsman and hired my brother. And that's how Gary's—or Byron's—career rocket ride began.

When he got there, the station was owned by RKO General, an American company. Canada's broadcast regulator, the BBG or Bureau of Broadcast Governors, precursor to the CRTC, eventually changed the ownership laws, forcing RKO to sell. CKLW, at the time, was on the cusp of becoming the biggest and most influential radio station in the world. I do not exaggerate.

The station was known as the Big 8, for its spot at 800 on the AM dial. It wasn't a clear channel, but the station had a flame-thrower of a transmitter, and all fifty thousand watts pumped that booming signal across eight provinces and twenty-three states. If the weather conditions were right and the signal skipped through the atmosphere, you could listen to CKLW halfway round the world in Finland.

The station was geographically in Windsor, but its heart and soul, and most of its audience, was in Detroit. And Detroit, like many American cities at the time, was a powder keg ready to explode. That summer, it did.

In July 1967, Detroit Police raided an after-hours club, known as a "blind pig." It triggered one of the worst race riots in US history. As Detroit's inner city burned, National Guard troops moved in to restore order. Five days later, it was over, with forty-one people dead, more than eleven hundred injured, and more than two thousand homes and businesses destroyed. It was baptism by fire for a nineteen-year-old from Calgary, still wet behind the ears in the news business.

Within a couple of years, Smyth had decamped and returned to Toronto to lead the newsroom and build his legend at 1050 CHUM. And though there was a more senior newsman in the station to take over at CKLW, Byron was picked to become the next news director at the Big 8, at the age of twenty-one.

When he took over the newsroom at CKLW, the station was ascending to the zenith of its industry dominance and influence. The story is well told by Toronto documentary filmmaker Michael McNamara in *Radio Revolution: The Rise and Fall of the Big 8*. It may seem unthinkable to a new generation of Millennials, but in those days, radio really mattered. There were no iPods, not even Walkmans, and FM radio had yet to control music programming over the air. Top 40 AM radio was where it was at. And nobody did it better than the Big 8. In fact, every station that was doing Top 40 was trying to do it like them.

The music drove the format, known as "Boss Radio" or "Drake Radio" after California programming guru Bill Drake. High energy, no pauses, no dead air. The program director at the station was Paul Drew, another giant of the industry. The station's sound was incredibly tight. The signal boomed, and the CKLW engineers had found some secret sauce for the transmitter that gave the signal muscle—not just in its reach, but also in the punch that came out of the dashboard speaker or transistor radio. Drew would speed up the turntables by a couple of RPMs so that the songs were shorter but not distorted. Because of that, CKLW was about to get two or three more songs on the air every hour.

And it wasn't just how many songs they played, it was which ones—and they played the right ones. The music director was Rosalie Tremblay, a lovely woman with an ear for what people wanted to hear. She rose from record librarian to music director and was the most influential person, man or woman, in the music industry. The songs she picked to play became hits. The bands and artists she put on the air became stars. Motown music would reach a wide audience thanks to her and airplay on CKLW. Detroit's Bob Seger wrote a song about her. She wouldn't play it; it just didn't feel right.

But the songs she did play were listed each week on the CKLW Big 30, the station playlist that would hit record stores on a Friday. It was the bible for the radio industry, a must-read for thousands of radio programmers around the world who wanted a little bit of the Big 8 magic on their air. The Big 30 pamphlet also helped me stay in front of the new music despite living in small-town BC (remember this was before iTunes and Google). Byron's secretary's job description included mailing me a copy of the Big 30 every week, and back then, Canada Post could get it to me in just a couple of days. I still have my collection of them, and it's fun to go back and see what the number one song was, for example, on the week of August 9, 1971. "Spanish Harlem" by Aretha Franklin; you knew.

It wasn't just the music or the jocks that gave the Big 8 its distinctive sound. Far from it. That kid from Calgary was rebuilding the CKLW newsroom, and he introduced the new concept of 20/20 News. The idea was to run the newscasts at twenty minutes after and twenty minutes to the hour. That way, when other stations interrupted the music at the top and bottom of the clock, listeners could punch the button on their car stereo to keep the music playing on CKLW.

More than the schedule, though, was the way the news was presented on the station. For music stations, news was (and is) considered a tune-out. Byron's goal was to make it a tune-in— and was it ever. Before long, 20/20 News was known for blood and guts, sensational writing and delivery. The sound effect of an old teletype machine clattered away in the background for further dramatic effect. Soon, listeners were hearing about "toes peeking out from under the rubber blankets at the Wayne County morgue," victims "strained through the grill of a Buick," and a man who attacked his wife with his "genuine, Willy Mays, Lightnin' Strike, Louisville Slugger baseball bat . . . hitting a thousand on the woman's head."

It was lurid, it was over the top, and it was a hit. Detroit at the time was known as Murder City, USA, so there was no shortage of fodder for the newsroom. And my brother assembled and led a great team, with the likes of Joe Donovan, who translated the tabloid flair to sports, Jon Belmont, Randall Carlyle, Lee Marshall, the late Mark Dailey, Keith Radford, and of course the master craftsman, Grant Hudson. That wasn't Jim Reese's real name either, by the way. I've always gotten a kick out of knowing that he was named after me.

When my brother hired him, they had the same kind of conversation that Dick Smyth opened with in 1967, when he told Gary to call himself something else (I'll explain later). They needed to figure out a new on-air name for the new hire.

"I have a brother named Hudson," Byron offered.

"Yeah, Hudson! And I've always wanted to be called Grant. I'll be Grant Hudson!"

The names on the CKLW team of that time are all synonymous with a style of radio news that might never be accepted today, but will stand the test of time. Interestingly, some of the critics of it were part of its inception, and though they might try to distance themselves from the 20/20 style, they still enjoy the attention and show up at all the station reunions. When he was challenged years later about it being sensationalistic, "yellow" journalism, Byron defended it as being the right thing for the time. And he was right.

It's funny about those reunions. For many of the people who worked at The Big 8 in the 1970s, it was the high-water mark. I liken it to veterans of the Second World War, for whom nothing that came after ever came close. CKLW is unique, and I think the Detroit radio market of that day is too. The people who were part of it, regardless of their subsequent success, can't top it, and they keep coming back.

It really was a Big Deal. I have a friend who grew up in southern Ontario who talks about summers spent at Ipperwash Beach, on Lake Huron. You could go for miles, and every car on the sand would have its windows or roof down, the radios in unison, blaring the distinctive a capella jingle sung by the Johnny Mann singers, "The Biiiig 8, C-K-L-W." It would be the same on hot summer nights in troubled downtown Detroit, the station providing the soundtrack as young people raced their muscle cars up and down Woodward Avenue.

I always felt like I lived that life vicariously. I'd had a couple of occasions to visit my brother, and we visited him as a family as well. I'd come into the station with him at 4:30 AM and watch the morning news run unfold, in slack-jawed awe. It's no wonder that, given my experiences as a little boy with my dad at CFAC and later at CKXR, and a taste of the Big 8, there was never any question in my mind about what my future held.

The other distinctive thing about the CKLW personalities in those days was the life they led outside the radio station. Many of the Big 8 jocks and newsmen (and they were all men then) lived at the Holiday Inn in Windsor. The hotel was built along the banks of the Detroit River, with balconies looking literally straight down onto the water. Across the river was a panoramic vista of downtown Detroit, now dominated by the Renaissance Centre's towers, which house the world headquarters of General Motors. From a distance across the river, downtown Detroit looks better than it does up close, on the ground. It has undergone a revitalization in recent years, but back then, it was a decrepit shell of burnt-out, boarded-up businesses and vacant skyscrapers, such as the old JL Hudson department store. Like thousands of people in the city, mostly white, Hudson (the store) had fled to the suburbs beyond Eight Mile Road.

But I have always thought it was too easy to turn Detroit into a punching bag. It is an interesting, exciting, important city. Some of that excitement may come from the danger that is also part of its character. Detroit's decline began a long time ago, and it will take a long time to bring it back, however far back it is able to come. The city has suffered from corrupt local government, and it has gotten pinched in the grinding gears of economic change. The optimism at the most recent Detroit Auto Show offers some hope. If you've never been and have the opportunity, you should take it in. Especially if you are a car buff—it's a kick.

Life at the Holiday Inn was a bit of a kick too. The hotel had a fourth floor that was partitioned into apartments, two-storey suites with a bedroom loft and floor-to-ceiling windows overlooking the Detroit River and Motor City skyline. And with the stars from the biggest radio station in the city calling it home, there was no shortage of overnight guests and parties. The place rivalled the Playboy Mansion in its day. The stories those walls could tell, but they took their secrets to the grave. Many years later, the old wood-frame Holiday Inn burned to the waterline.

By then my brother had settled down, living a couple of miles away in another two-storey apartment suite, this time in a high-rise condo with his new wife. They met when Jo-Jo Shutty applied to become CKLW's helicopter traffic reporter. She got the job, becoming the first woman in North America to do it. And she got her man. After a couple of years, dating led to an engagement, and they were married on February 28, 1976. Jo-Jo was and is a pistol, a diminutive blonde with a big head of hair, who speaks with a slight twang that tells you immediately she hails from the Midwest. A native Detroiter, Jo-Jo was a champion baton twirler and MSU Spartan alum who worked in Detroit television before joining CKLW. She and her sister, Sharon, a just-retired reporter at WMAQ-TV in Chicago, were raised in the Detroit suburb of West Bloomfield. Jo-Jo is still on the air in Detroit, providing traffic reporting for a network of stations.

As told in the *Rise and Fall* documentary, CKLW met its eventual demise as a Top 40 powerhouse thanks in part to the stifling CRTC regulation mandating a percentage of Canadian music on the radio. That was only part of it. By the late 1970s and early 1980s, music stations on the AM dial could no longer compete with the rise of FM radio.

Byron left CKLW and went "legit," you might say, leaving behind the lurid 20/20 News that he had helped create. He moved to WWJ radio in Detroit, anchoring mornings on the CBS News station. He also anchored television news, becoming the first newscaster on WKBD Channel 50, now the FOX affiliate in Detroit.

His success in Detroit broadcasting could be eclipsed only by another highlight of his career, "The Americans," a phenomenon that happened almost by accident. In 1973, a copy of an editorial crossed his desk. It was written by Canadian broadcaster Gordon Sinclair, who had read it on his daily program on CFRB radio in Toronto. The commentary was, in essence, a thank-you note to the United States, for all the country does to help others around the world (even if the gratitude is expressed with a kick in the teeth).

CKLW was required by its licence to provide a certain number of hours per week of so-called foreground programming, the kind of stuff that didn't really fit the format, and aired when few people were listening, on a Sunday morning. Byron contacted CFRB and obtained permission to air it in Windsor and Detroit, recording his own reading of the Sinclair editorial.

The response was overwhelming. The switchboard at CKLW blew up with calls requesting that the piece air again, and asking where listeners could get a copy. The message was just what Americans needed to hear at the time. The Vietnam War was dragging on. The Watergate scandal was shaking peoples' confidence in their leaders. The US dollar was hitting record lows. And people in countries around the world who had benefited from the generosity and compassion of the United States were revelling in its troubles.

The upshot of the Sinclair editorial was that the American Red Cross had already blown its budget for the year, broke after responding to one disaster after another, and in danger of becoming insolvent. A series of tornadoes had devastated the Midwest, and the Mississippi River was flooding. And yet, no other country was stepping up to help. It's no wonder the commentary struck a chord.

At that point, things moved pretty quickly. "The Americans" would be recorded and released by a Detroit label, Westbound Records. Byron met with Gordon Sinclair to obtain permission to use his copyrighted material. Sinclair agreed, on the proviso that net proceeds from the record be donated to the Red Cross, whose plight had prompted his commentary. This was agreed, and Byron went into the studio. His reading of "The Americans" was recorded with the backing of the Detroit Symphony Orchestra, performing "America the Beautiful."

The record was pressed and was in stores within a matter of days. It was a phenomenon. The single sold more than two million copies in its first month. By January 1974, "The Americans" had become one of the fastest-selling records in the United States, unprecedented for a spoken word recording. It went on to sell more than three and a half million copies. It was #1 in *Cash Box Magazine* and hit #4 on the Billboard Top 100. It spawned an LP with other original, similarly themed material.

Suddenly, Byron MacGregor was known and loved far beyond the reach of Detroit radio. He was interviewed by Barbara

Walters on the *Today* show, appeared on *The Mike Douglas Show*, performed on Don Kirschner's *Rock Concert* program, was introduced by Wolfman Jack on *The Midnight Special*, and made countless appearances and live performances. Other versions of "The Americans" were recorded as well. Gordon Sinclair put out a record of his own, on a Canadian label. It sold a fraction of the number of copies, largely because of Canadian distribution, but mainly because the message didn't resonate with people in Canada in the same way it did in the US. Also, even though they were his words, Sinclair's voice and delivery just couldn't deliver the message in the same stirring way. There was also a version by Tex Ritter, which had little impact.

Once the flurry of sales dropped off, proceeds were tallied, and true to his word, Byron donated all of the money he would have received to the American Red Cross. He and Sinclair appeared at the annual Red Cross convention in Minneapolis that year to donate their cheques. Backstage, Sinclair suggested he would make his a low-key presentation offstage, since the amount was considerably less. Not wanting to embarrass him, my brother agreed. They took the stage, and just before Byron was to present his cheque for one hundred thousand dollars, they played "The Americans." But they played the Gordon Sinclair version. It was like a punch in the gut. Still, a moment of incredible pride for him, and for us.

Even though he did not write the words, Byron MacGregor earned the admiration and affection of millions of Americans as a result of "The Americans." When US President Ronald Reagan made his first state visit to Canada in 1981, he spoke of Byron and Sinclair as figures who had given the United States an inspiring tribute in one of its darkest hours. Byron was recognized with numerous accolades and honours, including a declaration from the Michigan State Legislature, and the posthumous honour of the National Americanism Award.

He would later perform "The Americans" live, with President Reagan in attendance, at a ceremony in Detroit, where Reagan presided over a naturalization ceremony. Byron MacGregor was one of those swearing allegiance that day, proud to become a new American citizen himself. But he also remained a proud Canadian and held dual citizenship from that day on.

"The Americans" would enjoy a revival years later, following his death. It was revived after the terrorist attacks on September 11, 2001, and again after Hurricane Katrina, reproduced in print and airing again on radio and television. The difference, this time, was the internet. It spread even faster than in 1974, and so did the misinformation that accompanies so many stories online. Many believed it was a newly written piece, its original authorship and the real story of the recording muddled. There were even unsubstantiated claims that the Westbound Records release had not been authorized by Sinclair. That could not have been further from the truth. Don't believe everything you read on the internet.

Gordon Sinclair's son, Gord Sinclair, was also a veteran Canadian broadcaster, the longtime news director at CJAD in Montreal. Gord and I were good friends; in fact, it was he who nominated me for my first term as RTNDA Canada president. I asked him about the inaccuracies, and Gord told me that had his father not given his approval to the Detroit recording, he would have known about it, and he did not. If the elder Sinclair had indeed had any issue with "The Americans," I suspect it was because a man of his considerable ego did not like someone else's version of his work achieving greater success. In an interview with *The Globe and Mail* newspaper in May 1974, Gordon Sinclair said he was sick of hearing the record. I'm guessing he wasn't, that day on the stage in Minneapolis. Gordon Sinclair died in 1984.

When the hoopla had finally died down later in 1974, Westbound Records threw a party to thank the many people involved in the project. The company flew our family to Windsor for the celebration. Westbound presented several people and organizations with a framed display of three gold records, one for each million sold. My parents were among them, and the trio of golden 45s now hangs proudly in my home.

We were all so very proud of Gary and what he had accomplished. I think my parents worried that he was experiencing all of this too much, too soon. He had just turned twenty-six. And I can't help but think there was a tinge of regret for my dad, seeing all of his son's success and achievement, and fame, happening under an assumed name. My dad died later that year, but I think he and Gary had a reconciliation, if that's what it was or what it needed to be. In the end, they were on good terms, and I know they were proud of each other and loved each other very much.

Byron stayed at WWJ until the mid-1980s and then spent several years at a number of Detroit radio stations, including WLLZ and WOMC. He was still in demand as a public speaker and spokesman, and he and Jo-Jo devoted much of their time to community and charitable causes. He was a loyal supporter of the March of Dimes in particular.

Meanwhile, he suffered from several health issues of his own. In late 1994, he began to experience neuropathy. My mother was always convinced it was Post-polio Syndrome, because he had been successfully treated for polio during the outbreak in the early 1950s. He was at the age where such symptoms were appearing in many others. If that indeed was the correct diagnosis, it was one that was never made.

By December 1994, his health was failing, and he was admitted to Henry Ford Hospital in Detroit. Once in the hospital, his condition deteriorated. "Walking in the Air," the haunting theme from the animated special *The Snowman*, will always take me back to that time. Our kids were small and loved the show; it was playing in our house, over and over, as I was on the phone, first with Jo-Jo, then passing along updates on his condition to my mother and Leilani, and then trying to book a flight.

During the Christmas week, he took a turn, and my mom and I flew to Windsor, she from Calgary and me from Victoria, rendez-vousing in Toronto, to see him for what turned out to be the last time. Saying goodbye was heartbreaking. I bought a gold coffee mug in the hospital gift shop that I bring out every Christmas. As we sadly headed home, on our early morning flight from Windsor east to Toronto for our connections, we were blinded by a brilliant and beautiful sunrise. We took it as a sign. I can still picture it now.

I was home in time for New Year's Eve but wasn't much for celebrating. Then came the call, January 3, 1995. Gary Lachlan Mack, aka Byron MacGregor, was dead at the age of forty-six. In the end it was pneumonia and a systemic infection, likely caused by a hospital bug that antibiotics were powerless to overcome.

The trip to Detroit and the emotional hospital visits had taken a toll on my mom. So this time, Leilani and I flew back for the funeral. His death was big news in Detroit, and the funeral was a major event. Friends and colleagues, local celebrities and political leaders, and fans arrived for hours during the visitation at the funeral home. An overflow crowd of several hundred people turned out on a cold Monday morning, at a cathedral on Twelve Mile Road at Woodward, in the suburb of Royal Oak.

I was one of the pallbearers, along with his friends and colleagues. One of them was Edsel Ford, who was there for him nearly twenty years earlier, as an usher at his wedding. The eulogies ranged from the emotional to the hilarious—a lot of memories, and a lot of inside jokes that only some people in the pews would get. I delivered my tribute, barely choking my way through it, talking about a big brother who was truly an idol, a guy who loved to play Scrabble (how many thousands of games had there been?), who had a crippling handshake and a sick sense of humour, who had a great sense of style (he was always in a shirt and tie, the best-dressed man on the radio), who was a broadcaster of enormous talent and a great writer who passed on the craft to others, whose bear hugs were as big as his beautiful booming voice—a larger-than-life character who was kind and sensitive, generous beyond words, and whose caring heart had room for all. I don't think I made it to the end before I started to cry. When the service was over, many of his friends, and the CKLW alumni, gathered at a nearby restaurant for lunch. It was another Big 8 reunion. He had brought everyone together one more time.

As I write this, the twentieth anniversary of his death has just passed. I've been to Detroit a couple of times since. I have an affection for the city and everything about it, because it connects me to him, and it always will. Jo-Jo is still there, still covering traffic at WWJ and on the Metro Network. I don't stay in as good touch with her as I should. I keep promising this will be the year I do. We talked the other day on his birthday, and it was good to catch up.

If my dad's candle shone brightly and went out too soon, then so too did my brother's, burning even brighter and faster. He was one of a kind. My idol. I still miss him and always will.

# 11

## Crossing the Street

In the broadcasting business, it is known as "crossing the street." You don't always get safely to the other side. Fortunately, I did. But when an on-air figure who has been at one station for many years switches allegiance and goes to work for the competitor, there is no guarantee viewers will come along too.

When Bill Good and Pamela Martin were lured away from BCTV in 2001 to co-anchor on the upstart BC CTV, there was no spike in viewership. They did increase the ratings to be sure, but whatever dent they put into BCTV's numbers, it didn't shake the ground in Burnaby. It hadn't really occurred to me to do the same thing. But it turns out crossing the street was on my horizon.

At the CRTC hearing in 1999, into applications for a second Victoria television licence, there was no shortage of broadcast companies lining up for a crack. Among them was Craig Media, the Manitoba company that had grown from stations in Brandon and Portage la Prairie to the A-Channel network, with stations in Winnipeg, Edmonton and Calgary. They needed a presence in British Columbia. Later, the two Craig brothers, who inherited the business from their father, would expand into Toronto, with a station known as Toronto 1. But they bit off too much. The Toronto station was a drain on the company, and the A-Channels were eventually sold to CHUM.

CHUM was also bidding for the Victoria licence. The Vancouver shakeup wouldn't happen for a couple of years, and CHUM didn't have its hands on CKVU yet. CHUM had expanded its television presence with the acquisition of Ontario stations that became known as the "NewNets;" CKVR in Barrie became "The New VR," and CFPL in London was "The New PL."

CHUM won the Victoria licence and went to work creating "The New VI." Skeptics in Victoria were quick to point out there never was an "Old VI," so the name didn't make sense to those who didn't know about the so-called NewNets. There actually *was* an "Old VI," the heritage radio station CJVI, which was a sister Selkirk station to CFAC in Calgary in the 1950s and 1960s when my dad was there.

The outcome of the Victoria hearing was a concern to us at CHEK at the time. CHUM was a company with deep pockets that was good at what it did. We did some in-house market research and analysis, conducted by former BCTV news director Keith Bradbury, who was still doing contract work for the company. Ian Haysom, Rob Germain and I made several trips to Keith's retirement home on the Sunshine Coast to study his findings. It was like visiting The Oracle.

Keith had been critiquing us at CHEK, and he offered sage advice on ways we could prepare now for the eventual competitor, to maintain our market dominance. It turns out we didn't have much to worry about.

CHUM came to town with a flourish, setting up a temporary storefront operation across the street from a heritage building at the corner of Broad and Pandora, kitty-corner from Victoria City Hall, which would become the studios of The New VI. The historic brick building had been a church, a feed store, and, in recent years, a rundown furniture store. CHUM spent more than twenty million dollars restoring it, much of the money going to seismic refitting, the rest on state-of-the-art broadcast equipment and open-air studios. No expense was spared.

The building, and the broadcasts that emanated from it, were patterned after CHUM's iconic flagship CityTV studios at the corner of Queen and John streets in downtown Toronto. There were big windows so passersby could watch "the process." A signature "Speaker's Corner" coin-operated camera kiosk was on the corner, where people could get off their chests whatever they needed to, in the hope of seeing it later on television. What the camera captured, for the most part, were rants from late-night drunks.

The CHUM people christened the Victoria building "Pandora's Box." I'm not sure if they realized that in Greek mythology, Pandora's Box was the repository for all the evils in the world.

CHUM also embraced Nanaimo in a big way. The waterfront city about a hundred kilometres north of Victoria had wanted a TV station of its own, and many thought the CRTC should have granted the second Vancouver Island licence to Nanaimo rather than Victoria. The New VI built a storefront studio in downtown Nanaimo and originated its morning show from there.

The station went on a hiring spree, and when it signed on, and in the months that followed, The New VI was wildly overstaffed, with a reported 150 people on the payroll. Many of them were relatively inexperienced, and it showed.

The news director was Clint Nickerson, whom I knew indirectly. He had come from the CityTV newsroom in Toronto. My connection to him was the late Mark Dailey, a friend from his days in Windsor, when my brother had hired him at CKLW. Dailey had become one of Toronto's top crime reporters at City. I'd had sporadic contact with Clint over the years. We would occasionally do newsgathering favours for each other's shops, though we had no affiliation. Once he arrived in Victoria, we had no contact as competitors.

I knew they wouldn't come after me, as they wanted to be completely different. As their on-air hires were announced one by one, we were, at times, left scratching our heads. Never more so than the day The New VI announced it had hired Moe Sihota as its evening news anchor.

Sihota was a lawyer and career politician who was a polarizing figure in British Columbia. He had served in several consecutive NDP governments and had held several cabinet posts. He had also resigned from cabinet a number of times in the midst of various controversies. In 1995, he resigned as Minister of Labour when the Law Society of BC suspended his licence, finding him guilty of professional misconduct. He returned to cabinet the following year, but he resigned again months later amid allegations of corruption, abuse of office and conflict of interest.

The NDP government was defeated in a drubbing by the Liberals in 2001, and the NDP was reduced to a rump in the legislature, electing only two MLAs. For many, Sihota was the poster boy for an unpopular and scandal-plagued government that had been in power too long. So, it came as something of a surprise to us that The New VI had picked him as the face of their news department. But it fit the mold. The New VI was determined to be edgy and provocative. His co-anchor was Tasha Larson, who came to Victoria from Edmonton and was relatively unknown in the market.

Launching a new television station is a daunting undertaking. And as the September 2001 launch date loomed, it was clear The New VI wasn't going to be ready. A new launch date was set for the following month. "We open the door on October 4" was their slogan. What happened in the interim was a setback for the station even before it signed on. The New VI was not on the air on the morning of September 11, 2001, when terrorists attacked the United States. It didn't get a chance to show viewers how it could cover the biggest story of our lives. And when it did sign on early in the following month, the world was still in such a state of shock that for many, the launch went by largely unnoticed.

But it was hard not to notice. CHUM went all out with a lavish launch party. They closed off the block of Broad Street outside the station and threw quite a bash. The CHUM folks knew how to host a good party. Moses Znaimer was there, arriving by helicopter after christening the new studios in Nanaimo. The event was broadcast live, beginning with their evening newscast. A big crowd turned out.

We were watching at CHEK, with a little trepidation, perhaps. After our broadcast was over, several of us drove downtown and crashed their party. We didn't really crash it; they made us feel welcome. And we were more than a little envious of the facility.

CHEK was located just north of downtown Victoria, in a concrete bunker of a building that had been built by the CBC in the early 1980s. In its wisdom, after spending taxpayers' dollars to build a stand-alone Victoria station, the public broadcaster decided it wasn't going to open one after all. WIC bought the empty TV building, and CHEK moved in from its home in a Quonset hut on the edge of a suburban golf course. When I arrived in 1985, the station had only been in the new building for several months, and everything was still brand new. But by 2001, the CHEK studios, by comparison, were getting a little tatty.

The New VI studios were palatial, and bristling with the latest technology. Although they included some corny CHUM touches. The floor of the newsroom was emblazoned with a huge map of Vancouver Island. The second floor was an open space over the newsroom, so cameras could shoot downward onto the anchors as they walked from one location on the "island" to another. It probably seemed like a good idea at the time. (Later, I would learn how much had been spent on the expensive flooring, as we put down a new layer, covering up the map.)

The New VI tried a lot of different things. A Steadicam would follow anchors and reporters up and down staircases, into and out of edit suites, up onto the roof. Standups were perched on the corner of a reporter's desk, followed by a sprint to another location. Some nights the newscast was enough to give viewers vertigo.

Another innovation was weather delivered from a sailboat. I'm not making this up. The station hired a local salt, a folk musician by the name of Tony Latimer. His sailboat, the *Forbes and Cameron*, was equipped with a portable microwave transmitter so that he could deliver his forecast from Victoria's Inner Harbour, or locations farther offshore. Again, this probably seemed like a good idea at the time.

The newscast was frenetic. The storytelling and selection of content was obscure. The New VI tried so hard not to be mainstream that it drifted to the outer fringe. You could argue that this format might never have succeeded in a conservative, buttondown market like Victoria. That was part of it. But the newscast also had an amateurish feel to it. And the viewers who sampled it at the outset—many of them, at least—did not come back, though the station did have its supporters.

I say all of this gently, though, because the staff was made up of good people who, for the most part, tried hard. I would work with many of them later. And to its credit, CHUM had tried something new, and did what it said it was going to do.

As an anchor, Moe Sihota was out of his depth many nights. But he proved himself to be a very capable commentator. His political talk show with Norman Spector, the former diplomat and Chief of Staff to Prime Minister Brian Mulroney, was very good. Among the many local productions The New VI was airing, it was must-see. I was a regular viewer, and there were many others also watching *VILand Voices*. But there were not many others watching their newscast each night. In the months following their launch, we would study the overnight ratings at CHEK, beating them every night, usually more than ten to one or better.

We would poke fun at them—sometimes, unfortunately,

in public. I was emceeing an event one night shortly after their launch, and I joked about how scary it was watching TV news these days: "First 9/11, then the anthrax scare, and now . . . The New VI. When will it stop?" A year or so later, again at the podium of some event, I remarked how The New VI was marking its first anniversary, and to celebrate they were taking all of their viewers out to dinner.

"But it's not so bad," I went on. "They had to reserve a booth."

This got a good laugh, but not from everyone at the dinner. The New VI's General Manager and Community Relations Manager were there, and they did not appreciate my attempt at humour. I'm sure it must have caused an awkward moment at their table. I was genuinely sorry later to learn they had been deeply embarrassed and offended.

One especially memorable moment for us at CHEK came in 2002, when the Queen and Prince Philip came to Victoria, the second stop and first major event on her Golden Jubilee tour of Canada. I was particularly invested in the story, as I had been invited to host the welcoming luncheon for the Royal Couple the following day.

The Canadian Forces Airbus carrying them from Nunavut was scheduled to land at Victoria International Airport at about 4:30 PM. We had launched special live coverage of the arrival, beginning our newscast early, carrying a live pool feed from the airport. So did The New VI.

The Queen's plane landed right on schedule, as royal visits do. We came up hot on the air at 4:30 with a live shot of the Canadian Forces Airbus taxiing to the tarmac. So did The New VI.

What happened next became local news legend. I didn't see it live, because I was on the air myself, and we weren't recording their coverage (which we should have been), so it wasn't until later that I actually saw it.

The live shot from the airport came up and The New VI anchor Tasha Larson was providing the live narration. Several seconds went by before she spoke; all that was heard was the whine of the jet engines and the early cheers and hubbub from the throngs who had turned out at the airport to greet the Queen.

I don't know why it happened. I don't know if something had gone wrong in their coverage, or if she was getting bad news in her earpiece from a producer. But whatever the reason, as New vi viewers watched the Queen's plane fill the screen, waiting for her to emerge, the first word out of Tasha's mouth, yelled at the top of her lungs, was "FUCK!"

Our control room crew members, who had seen it, were incredulous, but we stayed focused on our own coverage. Someone got in my ear to tell me what had happened. Despite our stations' intensely competitive relationship, I felt bad for Tasha, who I didn't really know. It was a classic example of why anything you say with a microphone in earshot must be suitable for broadcast. You have to assume every mic is always live.

As an aside, any recorded evidence of the incident was well and truly suppressed at The New vi. When I eventually joined the station later, I was determined that this clip must be included in the Christmas blooper reel, even if it was a couple of years out of date. (Blooper tapes were apparently verboten in the first couple of years at the station.) It took some effort to locate a copy of it.

By early 2004, CHUM had had enough. The losses were mounting. There had already been at least one round of staff cuts. Start-ups are expected to lose money at first. But the situation was such that the new leadership at CHUM determined there needed to be changes in Victoria, fast. Enter Richard Gray.

Richard and I knew each other, though not well. Several years earlier, we had hit it off during the RTNDA Canada central region conference in Brockville, Ontario. The highlight of that convention was a pig roast at a mansion on the shores of the St. Lawrence River, overlooking the Thousand Islands. He was at CHRO in Pembroke, Ontario, at the time. This was another station

CHUM had acquired and rebranded "The New RO." I liked Richard. He was a smart guy, quiet and analytical, with a good sense of humour. He is a good newsman who understands the business end of the industry, and he has gone on to become one of the top broadcast executives in Canada.

CHUM sent Richard to Victoria to fix The New VI. He arrived in early 2004 and assessed the station, and its situation, and presided over his first round of staff cuts.

My first contact with Richard in BC came as a result of the regional RTNDA convention later that spring, which was being held in Prince George. I was not attending, somewhat to my chagrin, because the recently appointed GM at CHEK, Ron Eberle, felt Rob Germain should be there instead. I had wanted to go, since I had history in PG, but accepted the fact and was just glad that someone from our station would be there. Registration was flagging in the weeks leading up to the conference, partly due to geography. It was a nine-hour drive from the Lower Mainland, and for whatever reason, you could fly to Europe for about the same price as a return flight to Prince George.

I called Richard to welcome him to Victoria, and to encourage him to attend the BC regional. I didn't speak to him but left a voice mail. He called back and left a message right away.

My desk in the CHEK newsroom (or CH as the station was known then) was in a pod of workstations in the middle of the newsroom. I never did have an office, except for the time I claimed squatter's rights in Tony Cox's old office before Rick Wiertz showed up. My desk was a cluttered mess right in front of the assignment area.

I was clearing voice mails on speakerphone when Richard's reply played back. He thanked me for the welcome, assured me he was attending RTNDA and then said, "Please give me a call about a proposal I'd like to bounce off you." Every head within earshot spun around as I lunged for the handset to get the call off the speaker.

When I called him back, Richard invited me to dinner with him and Brad Philips, whom I had never met. Brad was CHUM's regional VP for British Columbia and GM at CityTV in Vancouver. Richard said they had a plan for the future of The New VI and would like to know if I wanted to be part of it. I agreed, and he suggested we meet somewhere discreet. "I'm not one for sneaking around," I told him, "but we can get together wherever you like." He told me Brad would be in town in the next several days and he'd let me know where.

They had a suite at the Fairmont Empress Hotel, with dinner delivered by room service. The Stanley Cup playoffs were underway, playing on a TV in the corner. There was a bar with cold beer and some snacks before dinner. We chatted for a while before the waiter arrived with our meal.

Keep in mind that I had been on the air in Victoria for nearly twenty years at this point, and had emceed and attended innumerable events at the Empress over that time. I know many of the hotel staff by name. When our server walked in and saw me in a private dinner meeting with executives from CHUM, his eyes were like saucers. "Gentlemen," I said, "I think our cover has been blown."

Fortunately, I suppose, I had been transparent with the CHEK management from the start. It never really occurred to me that I would leave the station to join the struggling New VI. I had told Rob Germain and GM Ron Eberle about their approach, and that I would accept the dinner invitation, but it was largely an intelligence gathering exercise to see what our competitor was doing next.

Over the course of the evening, chatting over a dinner of the Empress Hotel's outstanding rack of lamb, Richard and Brad told me why they had invited me here. The New VI in its first incarnation had failed. The losses were mounting; the news department, and by extension the station, had no credibility, and that had to change. They revealed they were armed with market research that made it clear what needed to be done. Phone surveys and focus groups all delivered the same answer to the question, "What can The New VI do to achieve credibility?"

"Hire Hudson Mack."

Sorry, I hate referring to myself in the third person. But that's what people were telling them. And they wanted to make it happen.

I offered my thoughts on where and how and why I thought The New VI had failed. I explained that I wasn't really looking to move. And I also touched on the fact that if I was frustrated at CHEK, it was the result of my inability to make the next step to news director, with or without staying on the air. This is what they wanted to hear, and they sent me off to consider the opportunity to rebuild a struggling news department: lead it as news director, anchor the evening newscasts, and become the face of a TV station I would help relaunch. It sounded pretty exciting.

But I wasn't sure.

I returned to CHEK the next day to essentially lay out their plan for my managers. And while I still wasn't really serious about crossing the street, Richard and Brad had gotten my attention.

I let a couple of weeks pass before getting back to them. If my manners were better, I would have been in touch sooner. But I still didn't know if it was the right thing to do. And there were distractions. There was a federal election campaign underway. And outside the newsroom, I was busy with the renovation of a rental home Patty and I had purchased. I was across the street from our house, gutting the basement to build a suite, up until two in the morning every night.

Finally, I screwed up my courage to reply to Richard. But I took the coward's way out and sent him an email. "Thank you," it said. "I am flattered at your interest and confidence. But I am not sure I have the stomach to tear down what I have spent nearly the last twenty years helping to build. I don't want to waste any more of your time. Best of luck." Or words to that effect. Then I hit "send."

Within minutes, Richard was on the phone. "I knew that was what you'd say," he told me. "Can we meet again?"

As it turned out, there were several CHUM honchos coming to Victoria, from both the television and radio side. Coincidentally, at the same time, CHUM was in the final stages of purchasing C-FAX 1070, Victoria's heritage news/talk station and its FM sister, from local radio legend Mel Cooper.

Richard invited me to breakfast, to meet with the CHUM executives and ask any questions I might have, or offer answers to any of theirs. I agreed and we met early in the morning a couple of days later. Around the table, along with Richard and Brad, were Stephen Tapp, CHUM's executive VP of television; Paul Ski, CHUM's EVP of radio; and CHUM's top legal and regulatory people. Heavy hitters. Breakfast didn't take long. Richard explained again why they thought I was the right person to help lead The New VI in a new direction. And they presented me with a written offer. I did my best to appear nonchalant as I looked it over. These guys were serious.

After the meeting, I went to work, and as I walked into the newsroom, I realized it had been a good idea to be up front with CHEK management about what was going on. One of the salesmen at the station had gotten a tip from his wife, who worked at the Laurel Point Inn, where I'd had breakfast with the CHUM representatives. "How was your meeting with the CHUM guys?" everyone wanted to know. The word was out. This really is a small town.

I met with Rob and Ron and, in a move I would regret later, showed them the written offer. It was at that moment I began to wonder if leaving CHEK was really going to be out of the question.

The response from my GM in one of several subsequent meetings was "We're not going to get into a bidding war or auction for you." I responded by assuring him that this wasn't about money, although CHUM's pre-emptive offer was far beyond what CHEK was willing or able to pay me, now or in the future.

No, I told Ron, this is about a chance to lead the news department, and to stay on the air. Something CHEK would never allow me to do, passing me over no fewer than four times as news director. Ron suggested a title such as "managing editor" to appease me. I explained to him that I was already Assistant News Director and had been since the late 1980s. It's also a matter, I told him, of CHEK giving me some kind of sign that it matters if I stay. Not bags of money. Just something. Anything tangible that demonstrated the station was willing to protect the equity it had built up in me.

Hell, I might have stayed put if they'd leased me a Lincoln. But he assured me that from the company's perspective, I was where I should be in terms of remuneration, with very little room before I hit the ceiling. I'd been well taken care of, I was told.

What galled me was that, as a commodity, I represented something that for nearly twenty years the station had invested in, and in which it had built up enormous goodwill. I was arguably one of the best-known media personalities in Victoria at the time, and I had distinguished myself with community service and charity work that reflected very well on CHEK.

It just struck me as bad management.

While all this was going on, Richard and Brad were waiting. They needed to pull the trigger on a deal soon if the relaunch of The New vi was going to happen in time for the fall season.

The back and forth at CHEK continued until July 2004. I was going on vacation for three weeks at the beginning of August, and I wanted some clarity before I left. Ron invited me to a meeting on a Friday afternoon at three o'clock. It was my last day before my holidays started. We chatted about the situation and he handed me an envelope.

"Is this your counter-offer?" I asked.

"This is our offer," the GM replied.

As I read it, I couldn't believe my eyes. Maybe it should have come as no surprise. As a counter-offer, it was a non-offer. Essentially the status quo.

"This is it?" I asked.

"This is it," Ron replied.

"Thank you," I said. "I'll give this my full consideration over my holidays." We smiled and shook hands. The meeting was over. And as I walked downstairs to the newsroom, I knew I was about to deliver my last newscast on CHEK TV. There was nothing remarkable about the show that night, at least not to anyone but me. Patty picked up on a cryptic hint I dropped as I signed off, but there was nothing obvious.

I then launched into a lengthy negotiation with CHUM. You always make your best deal going in. It took a couple of weeks to work out, but we had a contract agreement, the final stages coming in a phone call from the front seat of our van one morning on a camping trip.

Earlier in our holiday, while visiting my sister and mom in Calgary, I got a taste of CHUM culture. There was a voice mail on my phone, a message from CHUM President and CEO Jay Switzer.

"Hey, Hudson," he said, "just want you to know that we're aware of what's going on out there, here in Toronto, and we hope we can find a way to reach a deal for you to join us. Either way, thanks for your consideration, and please call me directly if you have any questions."

I wasn't getting any calls from Leonard Asper at Global HQ in Winnipeg.

But I was getting calls from CHEK and BCTV/Global. The first came on that Friday night before my holidays, and after my final newscast on Channel 6. Rob Germain called, concerned about my meeting with Ron Eberle and where we had left it. I had just finished telling my children, who were still quite young, that I was probably leaving CHEK for The New VI. Rachel had burst into tears. We were sitting in a circle on the kitchen floor.

Then Ian Haysom was on the phone, offering to help find a way to save the thing. But he couldn't give me the assurances I wanted or needed. If I was never going to be the news director at

CHEK, then what future opportunities might exist for me within our joint news operations? If CHEK was a farm team for BCTV, was I on the radar to replace Tony Parsons when he eventually retired? "Everyone's on the radar, and no one's on the radar," was the essence of Ian's reply.

It was too late to stop this train, and by now, frankly, I wasn't sure I wanted to. The feeling I got was that CHEK figured they had me over a barrel and I'd never leave.

There was at least one more call. Steve Wyatt was on the phone early one morning while we were at a motel in Penticton. I walked around the parking lot while we talked so as not to wake up the kids. But Steve offered no comfort. I was crossing the street.

Late in our negotiations, I dropped a bomb on Richard and Brad. Pretty much everything was worked out, except for a trip I had planned. Patty and I had escorted several cruises, in joint sales ventures between CHEK and local agencies. We had an upcoming cruise that had been promoted and was sold out, sailing from Vancouver to Hawaii in mid-September for twelve days. I told them that I understood entirely that the cruise was out of the question, but we may have to pay a penalty for me to break the contract.

Their response was another example of the CHUM way of doing business. Don't cancel the trip, they said. You could probably use it, since you'll be going flat out when you get back. They were right, and it was a lovely trip, but I couldn't relax, felt guilty I was gone, and was in touch by phone and email throughout the day, every day. In retrospect, I probably shouldn't have gone.

The work didn't stop onboard for a minute. One of the most important and pressing priorities was hiring. Richard had reduced the newsroom staff to a level from which we could realistically rebuild. In the interim, the nightly news block was essentially a half-hour cast that was repeated four times with updating and slight alteration. He had also cancelled weekend newscasts to save money. It would take years to bring them back. The news department was limping along until we could relaunch it in a new direction.

That took people. So, Hawaii or not, I was on the phone and Blackberry (which I miss) with potential recruits. Some former CHEK colleagues were already on the air at The New VI. Jason Pires had led the sports department from the start. Others would join us after my move. Moira McLean, Meribeth Burton, Howard Markson and Jonathan Bartlett were a few of the familiar faces now in a new home. We hired from elsewhere too, Stephen Andrew from Shaw TV and Shachi Kurl from Global. We also tried to lure Sophie Lui away from Global but she wouldn't join, instead coming back to co-anchor with Ed Watson at CHEK, before later returning to Burnaby.

We did a lot in little time. We changed the physical appearance of the newsroom, covering up the silly map on the floor and the corny slogans on the walls. We painted the room a neutral colour and cleared away the clutter.

We built a set and a news desk. And that was a big deal. CHUM has always held close to its heart the notion of a walking, standing news anchor as part of its ethos. But I had been adamant in my meetings with Richard and Brad. If they were hiring me to change The New VI, we had to give viewers the "me" they know. That meant suits and ties, and a desk. Other NewNet stations now wanted one too.

Ours was pretty cool. And it respected the open concept that CHUM had built. The newsroom/studio/control room is in a large L-shape. We put the desk at the corner of the L, and built it on a rotating turntable. This let us shoot in several directions, with the working newsroom in one shot, and the control room in another.

Not everything we did turned out the way we had originally planned. And that included the newscast itself. I was to have a co-anchor. And I did, for two nights.

The intended co-anchor was a woman who previously had a small on-air role, and after going through a final dress rehearsal, I began to worry that she was out of her element. We forged ahead though, and on the Tuesday after Thansgiving we went on the air with the new New VI. We realized that we were getting a rare chance at making a second first impression. And if viewers sampled it again and didn't like it any better than the first version, we were sunk.

We were all nervous, but we'd put together a strong lineup. One of the very good hires I had made was my old friend Dave Biro, who is one of the great broadcast journalists in the industry. Dave and I had worked together at CHEK before he had left to work in political communications at the legislature (he was part of BC Liberal leader Gordon Wilson's team—and that position had come about as a result of his work producing *The Judi Tyabji Show* at CHEK. Tyabji and Wilson, who later married, were tabloid fodder at the time, thanks to their initially denied romance.) Dave had been at CBC radio in Victoria when I hired him, but he is a true TV newsman and was ND at CKVU in the 1980s. He has great news sense, and no one is better than him at getting your news department ready to cover an event such as an election. Another former CHEK colleague I recruited was reporter Howard Markson, hired initially as a producer before we agreed his strength was on the street.

So, there we were on the night of October 12. The important thing was putting a clean show to air, which we did. It was a thrill to be finally launched. But after two nights I became more concerned than ever about the co-anchor situation. In my opinion it wasn't working, and to me it looked highly unlikely it was going to. I didn't feel we could take the chance.

There was some urgency in our situation. We needed to start strong, given the station's initial struggles. And more pressing was the fact that that night we were hosting a community and client reception to mark the relaunch and introduce our new on-air team. If we were to drop the co-anchor format, we needed to make that decision now, before facing our clients.

And the station needed new clients. One of the challenges

faced by the old New VI is that the ratings were so poor they couldn't attract many advertisers. We used to joke that Bob from "The Bead Shop" was the biggest client they had. He might have been. Making a good and lasting impression on community leaders and potential advertisers was crucial.

Richard and I got Brad on the phone. He was flying over later from Vancouver for the party that night. But we needed a decision now. He was shocked that we were already prepared to pull the plug on the co-anchor approach, but he concurred that we needed to address the issue now.

As we were preparing for what was promising to be a difficult meeting, I went back to my office in the newsroom, mid-morning, and all hell was breaking loose. Happy Valley Elementary School in Langford was on fire. Students were safe, the school had been evacuated, but there was panic among parents who were hearing the news but didn't know if their kids were okay. We had scrambled crews to the scene, which was a good half-hour away. We rolled our microwave truck, even though it was still only about eleven o'clock and we didn't have a noon show. Our next newscast was at five o'clock. I glanced at a monitor and saw Sophie on CHEK doing live cut-ins promoting more at noon. We matched the bulletins and our coverage of the fire that night was better than theirs, I thought. It was a good first test of our reaction to breaking news, and we passed.

But I was distracted by the meeting we were about to have. It went as well as you might have expected. My erstwhile co-anchor was naturally disappointed, and moved on to a different career within a few months.

I felt bad about the way that turned out. But everything was riding on the success of the relaunch, and it hinged on a newscast that clicked immediately. We quietly went to a single-anchor newscast that night, with a strong lineup led by a school on fire. The format worked, and we stayed with it for nearly a decade.

We had ripped off the Band-Aid. It hurts, but the pain goes away.

The other thing we did was launch a new morning show. New Day had originally been hosted by Bruce Williams in Nanaimo. Bruce also wore the hat of the station's community relations director, and his commitment to charities and the community was unmatched. He would attend or host hundreds of events each year. And we moved Bruce onto weather on the suppertime shows, using the segment as a vehicle to drive community involvement.

Bruce is an old pro who came to Victoria from London, Ontario, and adopted Nanaimo as his new home. The Harbour City has never had a bigger booster. Bruce had also done an earlier stint at CKLW, though it was after the heyday of the Big 8, and after my brother had left.

In the days and weeks that followed, we were on quite a ride. The reaction in the community was positive. The overnight ratings showed spectacular growth, though they had nowhere to go but up. Brad remarked that he'd never seen such a dramatic turnaround in a station's fortunes. Our salespeople were closing deals, and national advertisers were now buying. We were getting a lot of attention and earning new respect for the station. We steered it away from the fringes of the community and into the mainstream. On-air staff hosted or attended charity and community and business events. We were in demand as emcees, and we supported a long list of causes and events by buying a table or two. Things were going well.

And on the air we were breaking stories and breaking ground. We embarked on a run of awards that earned us more than fifty honours within a matter of a few years. Multiple awards annually from the Radio-Television News Directors Association in Canada and the US, including prestigious Edward R. Murrow awards. Recognition from the BC Association of Broadcasters, and a Jack Webster award, which is coveted by journalists in British Columbia.

We had also succeeded in subtly tinkering with the brand. We never used the term "Pandora's Box" anymore. Reporters were no longer "specialists," and The New VI, though still officially our moniker, was downplayed in favour of VI News. I liked it—and on Vancouver Island, there are no better call letters than CIVI. It wasn't long, though, before we changed our name for the first of many times. CHUM had purchased the Craig Media stations and was adopting the A-Channel brand they had started on the prairies. CHUM would rebrand the NewNet stations A-Channel.

For us, it didn't mean major changes to the set and the look, since we had just gone through the process. Our newsroom and look provided much of the template for the changes in the other stations. But rebranding a TV station is a big job. Changing the name and the look and the logo. Promos needed to be recut. Voice-overs re-voiced. News vehicles re-decaled. Everything redone, down to stationery and business cards. But it was worth the effort. And if The New VI had had any lingering negative connotation, we exorcized it with a new name and brand. Viewers may not have understood why the name A-Channel, but they liked it.

We helped launch our new identity with a road trip. The concept of taking the newscast on the road for a week had been perfected by BCTV in the 1990s. We had done it successfully at CHEK while I was there, but it was nothing like a Richard Gray road trip.

We had a bus, a big motorcoach wrapped in the new logo, with giant images of my face and Bruce's on the sides of the bus. We travelled for a week from Campbell River south, doing the newscast live from a different city each night. We also hosted a reception for local business and community leaders every evening. It was a great trip, and the shows each night looked fantastic. It was this kind of thing that our technical crew, including many who were there before me, excelled at. Live on-location broadcasts. Impromptu productions. We did big programs, like the live New

Year's Eve concert from Nanaimo that The New VI had done since its inception. I got to be part of only one.

New Year's Eve 2004 was the final countdown. We were in the plaza outside our Nanaimo studio (later rechristened in honour of Diana Krall). The headliner was Loverboy. I bought a black leather coat to wear onstage, though it was no match for Mike Reno's red leather pants. It was a fun night. We brought family and friends, and the plaza was packed. The show went off without a hitch. That's how our crew did it. But it cost a lot to mount a production of this scale, especially on a holiday, and the business model just didn't make sense. So that New Year's Eve was the final show.

The road trip was a hit, and it helped introduce us to many people in many communities. The challenge we faced was overcoming CHEK's nearly fifty-year head start, and the top-of-mind dominance and viewer habit that I had spent close to twenty years helping to create for them.

The difference, I think, was that we were having fun. And it showed. We'd try different things. We had money to spend (at least then) and we weren't afraid to do it. We had cool station swag to give away, and what better way to re-brand the station than give our clients and guests a Hudson Mack lunch box?

I wasn't sure if Richard was joking when he asked if I would be willing to put my face on one. It was a retro classic sheet metal lunch box, small and square with a handle and a clasp, like the ones kids used to take to school every day. We commissioned an artist to draw a caricature of me with the new A-Channel logo in a stylized monitor. On the other side was a cartoon-style drawing of Vancouver Island with our news crews here and there.

The lunch box was a thing of beauty. It really turned out well. And we filled it with logoed T-shirts, ball caps, golf balls, pens and pads. You name it, for a while we had it to give away. We ordered about twenty-five hundred of them, as I recall, and had to get more.

We gave them away at client and community receptions,

and people loved them. I was especially glad to give one to the Trailer Park Boys when they came to Victoria (they said it would be a good place to keep their dope). It was one of the best uses of station swag I've ever seen. People still talk about them and ask me for one. They've become a collector's item of sorts, though I occasionally see one in a thrift shop. My kids would never carry one to school. But I understand.

As the ownership landscape in Canadian broadcasting continued to evolve, we changed names again in less than a couple of years. This time we were simply known as A. But not just A. The corporate logo police were very strict, and it needed to include forward and back slashes, like this: /A\.

If viewers had wondered what A-Channel meant, they had no idea what we were up to now with a monosyllabic, single letter identity. Once again, we stripped ourselves of every vestige of our former name and began again. We kept the local graphic decal shop on speed-dial. It was all driven by the corporate food chain. I will not glaze your eyes over with the minutiae of the corporate ownership shuffle that happened in the mid-2000s. But in a nutshell, it went like this:

In 2006, Bell Globemedia purchased CHUM. It marked the end of an era in Canadian broadcasting. The Waters family in Toronto had owned CHUM since patriarch Allan bought the legendary radio station in 1956. It expanded into television, first buying a share of Barrie's CKVR, and later City in Toronto, investing first, and then buying it outright from founder Moses Znaimer. I never knew Mr. Waters, as he was respectfully known, but I knew of his stellar reputation for loyalty to his employees, and his standard of excellence. His sons, Jim and Ron, carried on after their father's death in 2005, maintaining his high standards, inside and out.

So, Bell buys CHUM and plans to keep the City stations (including the original A-Channels in Calgary, Edmonton and Winnipeg, which had now been rebranded as City), and would sell off the current A-Channels (formerly NewNets) and Access stations to win CRTC approval. The following year, Rogers Communications reaches a deal to buy the A-Channels and CKX in Brandon, as well as some other stations, which were part of the CTV deal with CHUM. The regulator approved that purchase, but the CRTC told CTVglobemedia (as it was now known) that it had to sell the CityTV properties, but could keep the A-Channels. The deal to sell us to Rogers was off.

Are you still with me?

They say that if you are in the media in Canada, at some point you will have worked for the late Ted Rogers. I guess technically I could include myself in that, briefly, except the deal never went through. It was in 2008 that CTV switched us over from A-Channel to /A\. But less than three years later, we would change our name again.

In the midst of all of this was the "Save Local TV" campaign, the fight between the networks and the cable and satellite companies over "fee for carriage" or "value for signal." You pick the euphemism. The issue was that carrying local stations was mandatory for cable companies, but they did not have to pay the broadcaster for the signal that they then sold to subscribers as part of a bundle. The specialty channels that were eating away at the available audience were paid for their signal.

As a result, the specialties had two revenue streams, subscribers and advertisers. Conventional TV, which is labour intensive and expensive to run, producing local news and programming, has only advertisers to rely on, and they were spending less. Add to that the US mortgage and banking crisis of 2008 and the global economic downturn, and it was a perfect storm.

In 2009, CTV responded with a series of sweeping cuts. Morning shows at the /A\ stations were cut. It was the second time since joining the station that we had been forced to cancel our morning show. Both times it was a terrible shame. Across our station and the others that were affected, 118 people lost their jobs—almost a quarter of the staff through the /A\ system. In

2010, Bell Canada Enterprises (BCE) swallowed up CTVglobemedia's broadcasting division, and by the following year, it had been officially replaced by Bell Media. All that was left was one more name change. At the end of August 2011, /A\ disappeared, and we and the others became CTV Two. So far the name hasn't changed again.

I'm not surprised people had trouble figuring out who we were. If our ratings growth stalled over that period, I blame a series of name changes and less-than-adequate local promotion. Nearly ten years after I had changed stations, people on the street would still say "Hey, it's the guy from CHEK." Or they'd be watching you on CTV Two, /A\, or whatever, and would think it was CHEK TV because of the familiarity of the heritage station.

We had a good run and we did lots of neat things, and we contributed to our community and helped people. But little by little, maybe some of the fun was starting to go out of it. I still loved my job, and moving to The New VI was the best thing I ever did. I used to compare going to work in those early days to a carnival ride that scared you a little, but when it was over, you just couldn't wait to get back in line to take that ride again. That's what each morning felt like.

I will always be grateful to have had the opportunity to work with so many good people over the years, folks like Ed Bain and Keith Wells at CHEK. Keith has enjoyed off-screen success as an inventor and entrepreneur, and Ed is truly one of the good guys in this business. Others who've gone on to major success include my former CHEK co-anchor Jill Krop, now in charge at Global BC, and Michaela Pereira, at CNN after reigning over morning news at KTLA in Los Angeles. Some people I was fortunate to hire, some I sadly had to let go, and a couple I was lucky enough to hire a second time. From early days and throughout, I enjoyed our staff in The New VI/A-Channel/CTV Newsroom. People like producer Stuart Adamson and director Kathy Donnelly, two of the key players in getting the newscast to air each night. Great reporters, news photographers and editors, whose work made our stories look so much better than the rest, my assistant Heather Kim, and, of course, Adam Sawatsky.

Adam is easily one of the most gifted storytellers I have worked with in broadcasting. He can craft a story and create a character, with a command of the language and turn of phrase that sets him apart. What might really be the thing that makes him stand out is that he listens. I've seen more of his stories bloom and turn in unexpected ways, because somebody said or did something, and he noticed.

Viewers came to know him as "Sparky," a nickname for which I cannot take credit. A previous producer named Cindy MacDonald would bellow it across the room in her Maritime accent, and I'm told he would cringe. That's all I needed to know to carry the torch myself.

It was by accident, really, that I started calling Adam "Sparky" on the air. It slipped out one night, but it stuck. And viewers responded. Soon, the end of his arts and entertainment segment became their (and our) favourite part of the newscast. I will always miss blowing up that TV, a weird inside joke made public, which people still ask me about today.

I have always been a big proponent of fun. One of the first things I told the staff when I got there was that we were going to have fun at this. Every day we are given a blank slate, a clean canvas on which to paint the day. We enjoy the freedom to be as creative as we want. To champion the issues we choose. To be fair and ethical. To do good things in our communities. If we can't enjoy that, we're in the wrong business.

I have always loved what I do, and what we do together in this team sport known as TV news. I miss it a little bit. And I love it still. Maybe I'm not quite done with it yet.

# 12

# God Save the Queen

I am, and have always been, a monarchist. I love the Queen. And a highlight of my career was meeting her and emceeing a luncheon in Victoria in her honour.

I'm not sure where my affection for the monarchy began. I think it might be because she reminded me of my mother when I was a kid. My parents met the Queen when the Royal Couple visited the Calgary Stampede in July 1959. My dad was among the local luminaries invited to an event to welcome them to the city. And what my mom later discovered was that while she was fighting the nausea and morning sickness of the early weeks of pregnancy, so too was the young Queen. Both were carrying a secret at the Stampede Parade that day. My mom, in her early forties at the time, was then about six years older than the Queen. The monarch was pregnant for a second time, and my mother a fourth. Less than nine months later, they would be in labour within days of each other. Prince Andrew was born February 19, 1960. I arrived six days later.

Our prenatal path-crossing and what some thought was a resemblance in youth and early adulthood might explain why

I used to like Prince Andrew. That eventually did wear off, but not my affection for his mother. I think the Queen is wonderful, and though many will argue that Canada should break free of the monarchy, I will never be one of them. Even during the dark days of Diana's death, I think the Queen has been a role model for the world, and I am proud she is Canada's Head of State.

At the risk of seeming overly enthusiastic, I must also admit to having a collection of portraits and pictures of the Queen. One of the most prized among them is a pencil sketch by renowned Canadian artist Myfanwy Pavelic that we bought at an art show my wife Patty organized, which raised money for a legal case to fight the closure of our children's school.

There are other pictures in my royal collection, and I am always on the alert for a copy of the portrait of a young Elizabeth II, the one that hung at the front of the classroom when I was a kid. Maybe that's the picture that reminds me of my mom.

All of this might help to explain why meeting the Queen and, more than that, being invited to host a luncheon welcoming her to Canada would be a highlight of my career and life. It was October 2002, and the Queen and Prince Philip were visiting Canada as part of her Golden Jubilee, celebrating fifty years on the throne. The advance work was done early, as it is on all of these trips. Her itinerary was laid out to the minute. There would be a brief first stop in the far north, in Nunavut, before their flight to Victoria, then on to Winnipeg, Toronto, Ottawa and several other cities in central and eastern Canada.

In the CHEK newsroom, we were making our plans early. Our evening newscast would begin a half-hour early so that we could cover the arrival of the Canadian Forces jet carrying the Royal Couple, when it landed at Victoria International Airport. The luxury of a microwave truck allowing for live on-site transmission was still a novelty for our small station. But we would have network resources at our disposal anyway, given the national interest in the visit.

In the midst of our pre-production and planning, an invitation to participate personally in the visit arrived on my desk. No one could have been more thrilled. It was communication via the various levels of protocol, delivered to me through Victoria Member of Parliament David Anderson, who also served as Canada's Minister of the Environment. Anderson would later be criticized in the media for choosing his own children to present the monarch with flowers on the airport tarmac.

Anderson's office was extending an invitation—a request, actually—for me to serve as the host or emcee at the luncheon to welcome the Royal Couple on their arrival to Victoria. I could not have been more delighted to say yes. But it was also unnerving. Despite the countless events I have hosted or emceed over the years, there has always been a twinge of nerves. I liken it to the adrenaline an actor summons when stepping onto the stage. It is not necessarily a bad thing. But for anyone, especially an admirer like me, the prospect of hosting a luncheon for the Queen, and not screwing it up, was somewhat terrifying.

There were many meetings. There were forms to fill out and security background checks. The Palace's advance team, the "Grey Men" as they had come to be known years earlier, were in Victoria to make sure everything and everyone was in place. I was checked out and passed the test. There were protocol guides, floor plans, scripts and to-the-minute itineraries to study, walk-throughs and rehearsals.

The luncheon was being held in the Crystal Ballroom at the Fairmont Empress Hotel, the pinnacle of venues in the British Columbia capital, now as it had been since the Francis Rattenbury-designed CPR chateau first opened its doors nearly a century earlier. I could not count the number of times Patty and I had attended events in the room, most of which I had emceed.

The Royal Couple did not stay at the Empress, however. The Queen and Prince Philip stayed, according to protocol, at Government House, the stately mansion in Victoria's Rockland neighbourhood, where the manicured grounds overlook the Strait of Juan de Fuca and Washington's Olympic Mountains. This is the Queen's official residence in British Columbia, and home to her representative, the Lieutenant-Governor.

The current Lt.-Gov. at the time of the visit was Iona Campagnolo, just in the position for about a year. The former Liberal MP and cabinet minister from BC's north coast had been named to the role following the retirement of the late Garde Gardom, a longtime Social Credit MLA and cabinet minister, renowned for his gregarious nature, keen sense of humour and impeccable fashion sense. Garde was a good guy.

I digress. But while I am at it, I should point out that the Queen's representative in Canada at the time, Governor General Adrienne Clarkson, did not consider Government House sufficient for her accommodation needs. On a previous visit to Victoria, Clarkson, a former CBC broadcaster, chose to stay at the Empress, rather than Government House—which, it turns out, is indeed fit for a Queen.

On the day of the luncheon, I was summoned to the Empress early in the morning for a final walk-through, to review last-minute changes to the program, and for a final security sweep. This was only a year after the 9/11 attacks, and security was extremely tight.

The Crystal Ballroom had never looked better; it was decorated to a level I had never seen. It was gorgeous even undressed. The ballroom was the centerpiece of the beautiful Empress, not cavernous, but large enough for a big event. The ornate mouldings, mirrored inset barrel ceiling and crystal chandeliers had been made even more beautiful in a multi-million-dollar restoration in the late 1980s. Outside the wall of double doors leading to the ballroom was the Palm Court, an anteroom that had also been restored to past glory. At the centre of the room was a cupola, and the acoustics under the dome made it possible to eavesdrop on every conversation beneath it, though that's bad manners.

After the run-through and final check, I went home to get ready and pick up Patty, who was already getting dressed and made up. We had to be back to the hotel about three hours ahead of the Royal Couple's arrival. They had flown into Victoria that previous afternoon and spent a quiet night at Government House, resting up for what would be a busy day.

When we returned, we were escorted into the ballroom, where we waited for the guests and Royal Couple to arrive a couple of hours later. There would be a meet-and-greet receiving line in the Palm Court for the VIP invitees, but there was no assurance that Patty and I would be included. As the minutes ticked down and guests began to arrive, there was a growing excitement in the room and a growing uncertainty for Patty and me that, despite my being the host of the event, we might not get a chance to actually meet her.

Finally, as the guests had filled the room and the people on the list to greet the Royal Couple in the Palm Court had been ushered into place, came word that the motorcade had arrived at the Empress. The streets along the causeway outside the hotel, and along Belleville Street, had been cordoned off with crowd fencing, and the numbers were now in the tens of thousands hoping for a glimpse, or more.

Then, at last, someone from the advance team arrived at our table and put us out of our agony. We would be given the opportunity to take part in the receiving line. We were escorted out of a rear entrance to the ballroom and taken around to the Palm Court.

It wasn't a receiving line as such, but groups of people, who would be introduced to the Queen and Prince Philip as they made their way inside. We were in a clutch of people near the entrance to the court and were among the first guests to be introduced to the Royal Couple by MP David Anderson. It is beyond me to describe the moment. The Queen entered the room as though lit by a spotlight. She wore a suit and hat, the details of her wardrobe choice carefully chronicled by the throngs of media, especially the

Fleet Street press accompanying the tour. I was struck immediately by her diminutive stature. At six-foot-two, I towered over her, though in physicality only. She was tiny even beneath her hat.

Protocol dictates that one does not repeat, nor reveal, the details of a conversation with the Queen. I would never—not that I could. As we were introduced, I was agog. We chatted briefly, but it was all lips moving and no sound registering in my ears. I can recall her voice and her genuine interest in our conversation, but for the life of me, I cannot recall a word she said. Maybe someday I will get hypnotized to see if I can pull it out of the recesses in my subconscious. I know it is in there somewhere. It was a thrill.

Once she and Prince Philip moved on to the next waiting group, Patty and I and were taken out of the Palm Court through a side door and returned to the ballroom, where I would await a cue to take to the dais and begin the program. There would be a wait of several minutes while the VIP introductions concluded.

What happened next has a gauzy kind of blur in my memory, though, at the same time, it is crystal clear, if that makes sense. I was cued to take to the stage, which had no podium, to begin the program. I summoned the room to its feet. Moments later, the two double-doors at the far end of the ballroom swung open. And there stood the Queen, awaiting my cue to enter the room.

Have you ever had a moment when the ambient noise in the background is muffled into silence? Where everything in your peripheral vision fades away? Not tunnel vision, but a focus straight ahead that blacks out everything else in sight. So it was for me for that fleeting moment. As she stood in the doorway, our gaze locked and time literally stood still. The Queen was waiting for me to tell her to enter. I get goosebumps thinking about it. What was a matter of a few seconds felt like an eternity, and in that moment I knew somehow to savour it. There are a handful of once-in-a-lifetime experiences for any of us, and this, for me—an ardent monarchist and true admirer of the Queen—is among my most cherished.

After that, the event unfolded with clockwork precision. The luncheon was served with the Fairmont Empress's "Royal Service," each table with its own squadron of serving staff in white tie. There was no head table per se, but the Queen and Prince Philip were seated at round tables with guests. Following the luncheon, the honoured guests left to travel kitty-corner to the BC Legislature, where Premier Gordon Campbell and his wife would welcome them, and the official function was to unveil a new stained-glass window in the parliament buildings, commemorating the visit and her jubilee.

While lunch was underway, the throngs outside had swelled. The streets around the hotel and legislature were cordoned off with crowd-fencing to keep the roadway clear and to keep the tens of thousands of people on the lawns of the Empress and the legislative precinct.

Also on the lawn, surrounded by the crowd, were the various live broadcast positions providing coverage of the event. My instructions were to make our way to the tent housing Global News at the far end of the lawn, for a live breathless report on the luncheon: what we ate, what she wore, what was said, who committed a gaffe. But as Patty and I emerged from the hotel, we knew getting there was going to be difficult.

We managed to get out of the Empress via a side door, through the old Porte Cochere, and somehow got through the fencing and onto the deserted Belleville Street. One of the RCMP officers who immediately spotted us turned out to be, lucky for me, a Mountie who had become a good friend over the years, Sgt. Bruce Brown. He, like the other officers on the Royal Detail, looked great dressed in formal Red Serge, like Hollywood's image of the Canadian Mountie, recognized around the world.

I explained why we were on the street and where we were trying to go. Bruce let us make our way up Belleville, to the centre walkway on the lawn of the legislature, leading past the fountain and statue of Queen Victoria, toward the front steps, where the premier and his special guests would soon emerge.

This is where the day gets even more surreal. As we began walking up the centre sidewalk, the crowd along the east side noticed there was movement in the VIP area—us! There was a murmur at first, and then someone recognized me, and there was a shout that led to a cheer—not for me and Patty, of course—the crowd thought it was the Royal Couple. Soon there was a roar spreading through the mob—before people finally realized this couple was not *that* couple.

We made our way past the fountain, then near the front steps, just as the Queen's entourage emerged. We were stuck inside the fenceline, with no way out and no time to find a way. At the front we were near the fenced-off media pen—overflowing with local reporters and camera people, and the aggressive British media accustomed to carrying stepladders and wielding sharp elbows to get the shot.

I'd had a similar experience with the Fleet Street types—and aggressive Mounties—on a 1986 Royal Visit, when Prince Charles and Diana were here to open Expo 86 in Vancouver and did a walkabout in Nanaimo. I was in a penned area with other reporters and camera people, near a pathway in a park, where Diana was meeting people and accepting flowers. She was just a couple of metres away from me, speaking to an elderly lady. I reached out with a "shotgun" microphone to try to pick up their conversation. Out of nowhere, an RCMP officer's umbrella came smashing down, nearly knocking the mic out of my hand. Diana may have been startled, because she certainly noticed, taking a long look at him, then me, before moving on. Until the Queen's luncheon at the Empress, this had been my closest brush with royalty.

Back on the lawn of the legislature, the reporters in the pen were incredulous to see Patty and me inside the fenceline. But there was no time to escape. The Queen and Prince Philip were now just steps away. Patty and I realized we were trapped—and worse, we were blocking an area where Boy Scouts and Girl

Guides, and other lucky youngsters, were gathered behind the fence to present their bouquets and posies.

We had no option but to crouch in front of the line. As we squatted along the fence, the Queen and Duke of Edinburgh greeted the children and accepted their welcoming gifts. Patty could not move. She thought he was going to offer a hand a lift her to her feet, like Prince Charming. Instead, he muttered some kind of quip and stepped over her lap and around her, as she knelt to get out of the way. She was crouched facing out, and he was facing in, with her head at crotch level. I wish we had a picture. Though it was unintended, I'm sure, his trousers could not have come closer had he tried.

The Philip gaffe watch was already underway, after he had earlier quipped on a Canadian visit, "If they serve me salmon once more, I shall surely start swimming upstream," or words to that effect.

The Queen was nonplussed as always, ever the pro. I do not remember what she said to me or what he said to her. I don't know if the close encounter had the same lasting impression on him or them as it did Patty or me. I sincerely doubt it. But I will never forget the day Queen Elizabeth and I locked eyes and her husband went nearly crotch-to-face with my wife.

After the Queen's event at the legislature ended, we had a couple of hours before a ceremony at which the Queen's Golden Jubilee Medals would be presented. The day was a doubly proud one for me, as I was among the recipients of the medal, a recognition of commitment to community. The Queen herself did not attend the ceremony; she had retired for the day at Government House.

In addition to the medal, recipients were presented with a certificate. I left both in the care of Patty after the presentation ceremony, as I had to catch a red-eye flight to New York for the Radio-Television News Directors Association (RTNDA) Edward R. Murrow national awards. Years later, our station would be honoured with one, the only local Canadian station so recognized that year, though we have received dozens of them at the regional level. The Murrows are considered the pinnacle of awards in broadcast journalism. I was still on the board of directors of RTNDA International at the time, representing the region including Canada and all countries outside the US on the American board. It was a pretty heady day.

As Patty dropped me off at the airport, my parting words (other than I love you) were to please take care of the medal and certificate. She went to a friend's home for dinner after I left, and they celebrated our day in my absence. Little did I know until later, that the certificate got a lot of attention—and handling—at the dinner table. Patty was aghast to get home and find it was spattered with gravy. In a scene that must have looked like something out of *I Love Lucy*, she vigorously washed the parchment. But rather than remove the gravy, it just made the stain worse and began shredding the paper. She then tried to iron it to dry it out, but that made it even worse. We ordered a replacement from Rideau Hall in Ottawa.

# 13
## RTNDA

**B**roadcasting has given me the chance to meet many people, to go to places I wouldn't have otherwise had the opportunity to visit and to make very good lifelong friends. Much of that is thanks to my involvement with the Radio-Television News Directors Association (RTNDA). It has since altered its name and acronym to embrace new media, and is now known as the RTDNA, Radio-Television Digital News Association. If you've noticed me using both acronyms, that's why.

RTDNA serves an important role in guarding the ideals of journalistic excellence, ethics and press freedom in Canada, just as the international association does in the United States. Its annual awards program showcases the best work in electronic journalism; its conferences and programs provide newsroom leaders with professional development; and its networking opportunities foster a healthy, thriving community of broadcast journalists.

I have been a member of RTDNA Canada since 1989 and am now a life member after receiving the association's highest honour, The President's Award, in 2013. My involvement with the association began almost by accident, although I always knew of it and held it in high esteem, after my brother was a member years earlier at CKLW. I attended my first RTNDA convention in Whistler in 1990. Our news director at CHEK was the president of the association that year, but he chose not to attend, because he had just parted company with the station. So I went in his place. By the end of the conference, the so-called "rubber hose committee" had had its way with me, and I found myself elected to the board of directors, as the BC regional director of television.

I would remain on the RTNDA board for the next eighteen years, holding just about every position there was, including two terms as national president, from 1995 to 1997. And it was unfortunately on my watch that the association nearly descended into insolvency, though I cannot entirely take the blame for that. We had entered into a two-year agreement to hold joint conventions with the broadcast management association, the Canadian Association of Broadcasters (CAB). This was in response to a membership survey that showed a majority wanted to try meeting with the CAB. But the result was that our convention dates had to move, attendance flagged and the national conference, which is one of the major sources of revenue for the association, lost money. We were also nickel-and-dimed by the CAB, and our conference costs skyrocketed. The experiment ended badly for RTNDA, and that, combined with several other factors, left the association in a precarious position for a time. But we were able to step back from the edge of the cliff and restore its financial health. I give full credit to my friend, colleague and fellow board member Gerry Phelan, who succeeded me as president.

My involvement with RTNDA also opened the door to another facet of my service to the industry, of which I am proud. Since 1997, I have served on the Canadian Broadcast Standards Council (CBSC). The council is a self-regulatory agency created by Canada's private broadcasters through the CAB. It administers codes of ethics, conduct and broadcast standards established for the industry. The CBSC deals with complaints from listeners and viewers about a variety of broadcasting issues and programming content.

The CBSC was incorporated in 1990 and began administering the RTNDA Canada code of ethics in a decision made at the 1994 national conference in Victoria. Over the years, the council has made many decisions and has established jurisprudence, broadcasting case law if you will, which it uses to weigh the merits of audience complaints.

Its first high-profile decision, at least in terms of getting noticed by the public, dealt with the *Power Rangers* children's program, and a complaint about violence. Other cases that have piqued the public interest over the years have included *The Bugs Bunny Show*, and how the cartoon dealt with gender portrayal. Most recently, the CBSC was in the news over the reversal of a regional decision against the Dire Straits song, "Money for Nothing," and a complaint over its use of the term "faggot."

Though these high-profile and unusual cases may get more attention than others, the CBSC has served Canadians well in establishing and maintaining standards of acceptability on the air, whether it is profanity, nudity, fairness or violence. The council serves a valuable purpose, and I am proud to sit on its national executive.

It's through the CBSC that I have also made a very good friend in Ron Cohen. Ron recently retired as the CBSC's national chair. Ron is a Montreal lawyer whose CV includes everything from taking on the Mafia to producing Hollywood hit movies. He guided the CBSC from its infancy to maturity, and his elegant command of the language has resulted in well-thought-out written decisions, which will guide Canadian broadcasting standards and practices for years to come. These days, Ron and his wife, Wendy, spend much of the year in Florida, escaping Ottawa's winters. I will always have fond memories of our meetings and lively discussions, and wonderful evenings with the board at their beautiful home in Manotick (which, by the way, Ottawa cabbies could never find in the days before GPS).

I represented Canada on the international board of RTNDA, in Washington, DC, from 2002 until 2008. When I joined, the US association was in a period of change. I am reluctant to call it a time of crisis, but they were difficult times.

The US association held its 2001 national conference in Nashville, and it was scheduled to begin on September 11. I did not attend the conference that year, so did not see for myself how the day unfolded there. Imagine getting most of the television and radio news directors and managers in one place, away from their newsrooms halfway across the country, on the day of the biggest story in their lifetime. Then, make it so they have no way to get home in a hurry to lead their station's coverage. That's what happened to the three thousand odd news people, convention delegates who watched in horror on 9/11.

The board met briefly that morning, and realizing that the conference could not proceed, voted to cancel it. The financial ramifications were enormous, cancelling hotels and meeting spaces and refunding delegates' registration fees, but this was eventually resolved with the insurer.

Because of Nashville's generally central geographic location, some news directors had driven, so at least they had vehicles. But within hours, virtually every car rental company in the city had been cleaned out. There were no flights for days, and news directors were in a panic to get home.

The loss of the Nashville conference accelerated RTNDA's plans to join the National Association of Broadcasters (NAB) in a concurrent convention in Las Vegas in April each year. This partnership was very successful, attracting news managers to the huge NAB convention, which drew more than one hundred thousand delegates annually. If there was a downside, it was that the RTNDA convention and its exhibit floor seemed puny by comparison. Any conference would have.

The US association had previously held its annual convention in the fall, usually early September, and the location of the conference moved around the country to different cities each year. I had attended several conventions in the mid- to late 1990s, when I held a number of positions on the Canadian board.

RTNDA Canada also moved its annual conference around the country, and held smaller regional conventions as well. In my nearly twenty years on the board, I have had the good fortune to visit Canadian cities from one end of the country to the other, and to sample local hospitality at the regional events.

My first international conference was in San Antonio, Texas, in September 1992. As convention chair of the 1994 Canadian national conference in Victoria, I went to the international to get a better idea of how such a large event was organized. Patty joined me for this conference, along with our daughter, Rachel, who was about eight months old at the time and already a handful. Actually, San Antonio was a turning point for her. She was a quiet, effortless baby on the way down, and a wild child by the time we flew home. It might have been the food in a Tex-Mex restaurant one night, Rachel in a high chair at the end of a long table full of grownups. By the end of the night, there was a knee-deep pile of cheese, chips and salsa, and who knows what else beside the baby seat. She would never be the same.

It was a great convention and my first exposure to the American members. Our hotel offered babysitting service, but Patty was not comfortable leaving Rachel (neither was I, really, being nervous new parents and all). Years later, with Hamilton and Sheldon, we might have done it.

These were still the days of lavish spending by networks and suppliers, which hosted hospitality suites, and one of the favourites was the nightly party put on by the Tobacco Institute and its representative, Walker Merriman. The suites really don't exist anymore, at least not like that. The tobacco party was known for singing (and smoking), and the few Canadians fortunate enough to attend the US conference always made a point of wrapping up the night with a rousing rendition of "O Canada."

This was also when the CNN party was earning its place as a highlight of the conference after-hours schedule. In San Antonio, the network hosted a Texas barbecue and hoedown that people still talk about. At the time, CNN was still owned and operated by Ted Turner, who was then married to Jane Fonda. Guests were fitted with cowboy hats and margaritas on the way in, and the party went from there.

I would love to tell you I had the time of my life, but I can't. Patty and I decided instead to sample some of the entertainment options that were offered for spouses and families, and we took Rachel on the excursion to Sea World. And after a half-hour bus ride to the whale show, as the buses were leaving the parking lot and we made our way to the poolside arena, I knew I had made the wrong call. Maybe it was because I was imagining what I was missing, but the show seemed like it would never end. Finally, the buses returned and took us back downtown, just in time to hear the stories about what we had missed: margaritas with Ted, dances with Jane.

One of the other things that stands out in my memory of San Antonio was the night of the Paul White Award ceremony—the gala wrap-up event of the conference. (That night, Patty stayed with Rachel, exploring the River Walk and nearly pushing the baby buggy, unwittingly, into a bad part of town.) The recipient that year was American broadcasting legend Paul Harvey. Now, the rest of the story.

The Paul White Award is RTDNA's highest honour, recognizing a lifetime of excellence in broadcast journalism and service to the industry, named in memory of the first news director at CBS. The dinner was a thrill for me, rubbing elbows with the big names and major players in the industry, and just being there to see Paul

Harvey honoured. (Working in Prince George, it used to be one of my duties to edit the feed of his midday newscast, famous for its pregnant pauses. Occasionally, I would edit a few extra seconds of dead air into his pause for further dramatic effect.)

When the dinner was over, there was a post-event reception featuring the tallest and most delicious margaritas I ever tasted. After sampling a couple and soaking up the scene, I grabbed two drinks to go, to take back to the hotel for Patty. Tall, frosted glasses with perfectly salted rims, filled to overflowing. It was about six or seven blocks back to the hotel, but I walked with enormous care, so as not to spill a drop. And I didn't. Not a drop. I made it back to the hotel room to present Patty with a beautiful drink over which I would tell my stories of the evening. I had no sooner set the glasses on the counter, when my darling wife made a sweeping gesture, sending one of them flying across the room. Broken glass, tequila and lime showered the hotel room. We shared the lone survivor, and by that point in the night, a half a glass was probably all I really needed.

Many of the people I met in San Antonio that year were still active in RTNDA in the US when I joined the Washington board eight years later. Representing Canada was an honour. The semi-annual board meeting schedule of the day also gave me an opportunity to visit Washington, DC, once or twice a year. I have gotten to know the American capital quite well and love the city. If you have never been, you should put it on your list. Same with Ottawa and, for that matter, Victoria. Maybe I have something about capitals.

Professional associations serve a valuable purpose in protecting and fostering high ideals. And perhaps even more important, in creating and nurturing a community. Having friends and colleagues with a common purpose and shared values, and mutual challenges, is invaluable. I also believe in the value of awards, and the RTDNA awards program in Canada and the US is second to none. The RTDNA Canada regional and national awards are a showcase of journalistic excellence, and around the world the US RTDNA Edward R. Murrow Award is the gold standard. How proud I am to have helped lead our team at CTV Vancouver Island to dozens of them while I was there. The trophy case is literally overflowing.

What fills me with even more pride is an award I helped create while serving on the RTNDA Canada board. In Canada, the individual awards are named for industry luminaries, some post-humously. The best newscast award for television and radio is the Bert Cannings Award, named for the TV news pioneer at CFCF in Montreal. But there was not as strong a connection between Bert and radio.

So, in 1995, following my brother's death, I proposed to the board that the best radio newscast award be renamed the Byron MacGregor Award in his memory. My good friend Terry Scott supported me in the motion, and it was approved. Gary's widow, Jo-Jo, was in Toronto that year for the inaugural presentation of the Byrons, and she joined us again in 2013 to present the awards, and to be there as RTDNA Canada awarded me its highest honour, the President's Award.

That was a night I will never forget, with Patty and Rachel and Sheldon there with us. Hamilton was travelling in Europe at the time, and I wish he could have been there too. The night was highlighted (for me) by a tribute video produced by Heather Kim, who succeeded me as news director at CTV in Victoria. The video includes kind words from colleagues and giants of the industry, including Lloyd Robertson and Dan Rather, two of my broadcast heroes, who I am proud to also consider as friends.

I will always be grateful for the opportunities and friendships RTDNA has given me. My service to the organization, and through it to the industry, is a highlight of my career.

# 14

# Hail to the Chief(s)

My RTDNA board experience opened doors to me that I would otherwise never have stepped through.

In June 2005, the board met with President George W. Bush at the White House. This was the first meeting a sitting president had held with the RTDNA board since a 1977 sit-down with Jimmy Carter. This meeting came after many, many requests, and it was a breakthrough, given the relationship between the Bush White House and the news media, the Iraq War having faded the patriotic blush that came after 9/11.

The board prepared carefully for the meeting. The rules were set. There was a pecking order for board members to ask a question, after the president had addressed the group. We knew not everyone would get to ask theirs. When the President's advisors indicated time was up, RTNDA president Dan Shelley would ask the default final question. Because our group was large, the meeting was held in the Eisenhower Executive Office Building, huge and ornate, just south of the White House, built in the late 1800s. It is part of the White House complex and houses many of the staff members who work at the presidential residence.

When we arrived in the wood-lined meeting room, it had the feeling of a school field trip. But in our class were many of the leaders of broadcast journalism in America, a lineup of heavy hitters. Before the president arrived, we took our places in a receiving line of sorts for introductions and a photo. After that, we were seated at a large boardroom table set up in a hollow oblong.

I admittedly came to the meeting with a preconceived notion of President Bush. Though I did not indulge in the derision so popular at the time, like many, for me he did not seem especially bright, if I may be so blunt. I came away with a changed opinion. I believe Bush suffered in office from an inability to articulate his thoughts when speaking in a formal situation. In this setting, he was sharp, well-spoken, gregarious and charming.

Not unlike my introduction to the Queen, I admittedly am sketchy on the specific details of our small talk during the introductions. He had done his homework about us. I do recall him making note of the fact I was from Canada. (My Newfoundland friend Gerry Phelan was also there in his capacity as International Representative, a board seat that would later be rolled in with the Canada region.)

After the initial pleasantries and photograph, we took our seats. As it turned out, I sat directly across from, and one seat to the right of, the president. Because he is right-handed, he seemed to favour that side of the room when speaking, and as a result was looking directly at me during much of the meeting, often smiling to underscore a point. I liked him and gained new respect.

He declared himself to be a "First Amendment Guy," speaking about his view of the importance of free speech in an open society. "A free society is where people feel free without retribution to speak," he told the board. "A good society is one where information flows to the people."

But he went on, "There is a struggle between what the public should know and what should be kept secret, particularly with regard to national security. There's some information which could damage our ability to collect information, and that's where the real rub has been so far from my perspective."

I liked what the president said about the importance of the local news. "In all due respect to the national pooh-bahs," Bush said, "most people get their news from local news. And if you're trying to influence opinion, the best way to do it is to travel hard across the country and give the people their dues."

He may have been a First Amendment Guy, but the president would not endorse a bill before Congress at the time, the Free Flow of Information Act, which would protect journalists from being forced to disclose unnamed sources in federal court. This was the nub of our closing question to come from RTDNA President Shelley.

The president was also in the midst of his campaign for a social security overhaul, and he spoke at length on that. As the meeting continued, I was becoming increasingly aware of the clock and was waiting for presidential communications counsel Dan Bartlett to signal that our time was up.

Next question. Just one more before me. It was my friend from the board, Coleen Marren, the news director at WCVB-TV, the number one newscast in Boston. I forget what she asked, but it launched the president into another lengthy discourse on entitlement and his vision for the future of social security in America.

In our pre-meeting, which played out like a military briefing, we were given strict instructions not to follow up with any supplemental questions. You got one shot, that's it. But Coleen must have forgotten. I can't really blame her. Like any good journalist, she went at the president a second time, as he must not have answered her question the first time. But I was next, and she'd already asked her question, dammit!

If her first question had elicited a long-winded response, Coleen's follow-up produced what felt like a filibuster. I looked across the table at the so-called Leader of the Free World with pleading eyes. Please, stop talking, I have a really good question and this is my chance.

As I rehearsed it in my head again, just one more time, my palms turned cold and clammy. I reached for the cocktail napkin under my water bottle to wipe them. But I remembered I didn't want to wreck it. A cocktail napkin with the presidential seal would make a good souvenir.

The question, the question . . . don't get distracted by White House napkins. It was actually a pretty good one, I thought. Canada–US relations were a little fractious at the time, even by good neighbour standards. The recently appointed US ambassador to Canada, David Wilkins, had made a less-than-good impression north of the border. The southern Republican, Speaker of the South Carolina legislature, admitted in a CBC interview after his appointment that he had visited Canada once, though he couldn't remember where—the Falls? Nor could he name the Canadian provinces, which you may or may not think is a big deal. Geography aside, Wilkins was seen in Canada as a hardliner on trade and protectionism during the softwood lumber dispute, calling for trade sanctions against Canada during his time in South Carolina. He would later quite publically scold Prime Minister Paul Martin for his position on global warming.

He succeeded Ambassador Paul Cellucci, who had managed to alienate himself from many Canadians despite the feel-good hands-across-the-border glow and extraordinary bilateral cooperation that initially followed the 9/11 attacks. Cellucci was openly critical of Canada for opposing the US-led invasion of Iraq.

In a speech to the Economic Club of Toronto, he said America would never hesitate to support Canada if it faced a security threat. Critics reminded him of the First and Second World Wars, and the years-long delay by the US to join the British Empire on the battlefields of Europe and elsewhere. Canada also declined to join the US missile defense program, adding a further chill to the increasingly frosty relations. Anti-American sentiment was running high in Canada. The Liberals under Paul Martin had won a minority government the year before, demonizing Conservative leader Stephen Harper as "pro-American." None of this was lost on the folks at the White House.

I looked up. The President was wrapping up. Coleen wouldn't dare ask a third question. Would she? My moment had arrived. With my heart pounding in my ears, I was ready to ask. "Mister President, I am here representing electronic journalism in Canada; thank you for the opportunity to speak to you today. We have enjoyed a great relationship as good friends and neighbours, but there is some new tension across the border. Does the recent appointment of David Wilkins to replace Paul Cellucci as Ambassador to Canada signal a hardline in bilateral relations?" Or something to that effect. Yes, it's wordy. I know.

We would never know the answer, because I never got to ask the question.

Just as I was about to take a deep breath and launch into a hard-hitting diplomatic inquisition, Dan Bartlett stood up. "We're out of time, I'm afraid, just one more question." I should have seen it coming. Team player that I am (did I have any choice?), I demurred to President Dan, who delivered the closer. Minutes later, it was over, my question hanging in unasked immortality.

For his part, Bush seemed to be enjoying himself and was oblivious to the time. I'm sure that if he'd had his way, he'd have stayed until we were all out of questions. And I wasn't the only one who didn't get a chance to ask. But coming that close, without getting off a question, was tough. After he left the room, we sat in stunned silence for a moment, drinking in what had just happened, being part of history, at least RTNDA history. The meeting was a success. And if I may gush a little, it was a thrill.

Because of the size of our entourage, we had been broken into smaller groups for a brief tour of the White House. The security was very tight. There had been an extensive pre-meeting clearance, with thorough background checks. We had each been issued a visitor pass with a large "V" hanging on a lanyard, and we entered the White House grounds through the security shack on Pennsylvania Avenue.

My tour would end a little differently from the others'. As we were being escorted past "The Beach," the network standup positions on the North Lawn of the White House, I paused for a moment to make a call and send an email. We had made arrangements for me to do a pre-recorded hit for our evening newscast in Victoria, describing the meeting. We'd made arrangements with a CNN crew (we were a CNN partner and client) to do the hit. I wasn't sure if it was happening here or at their rooftop location a couple of blocks away. By the time I had made the call and figured out where to go, my group was gone, and I was alone on the grounds of the White House.

I wandered back to the West Wing to look for my people, but they were nowhere in sight. I made my way into the White House press room. Like you, I'd seen it countless times on television, with the president or the White House press secretary at the podium in front of the familiar blue curtain. Like most things, it is smaller than it appears on television, barely bigger than a decent-sized living room. The podium at the far western end, theatre-style seating for forty-eight reporters (seat assignment by network and individual pecking order), and the cameras and video and audio switching boards at the far end of the room. Smaller in person, yes, but not underwhelming. As I nosed around, a few technicians were working, oblivious to me despite the big, bright V-for-visitor tag swinging from the lanyard around my neck. Someone took a picture for me on my phone; this was before we had all discovered selfies.

The room was in the process of being torn down and temporarily relocated. It was built during the Nixon administration, overtop the White House swimming pool, which had been built with a public fundraising campaign in the early 1930s for

President Franklin D. Roosevelt. Beneath the floor of the press room, the pool is still intact and in good shape. Appropriately, perhaps, the lectern is located over the deep end.

In 2000, the room was renamed the James S. Brady Press Briefing Room, in honour of press secretary Brady, who was wounded in the assassination attempt on President Ronald Reagan. In 2007, the room was reopened, with modern digital technology and ergonomic seating. Reporters say it is still cramped.

But there I was, standing at the podium, the White House crest behind me and the presidential seal on the podium in front of me. It was a moment. I wandered around a little, and didn't try to go anywhere I knew I shouldn't, but I went largely unnoticed. Until I tried to leave.

I had made arrangements to go to the CNN camera location on the roof of an office building on I Street, just a block or so away, near Lafayette Park across from the White House. Next to the East Lawn, it is one of the most familiar camera shots on television. We had booked a satellite feed for a pre-taped hit that would air on our newscast in Victoria that night.

I returned to the Secret Service security shack on Pennsylvania Avenue and went inside to surrender my visitor's badge. The agents huddled around the closed-circuit screens were beside themselves, and rightly so, I suppose. (Keep in mind, this is the same Secret Service shack where agents later failed to notice an intruder jump the fence and make his way inside the White House.) Had I been there with malicious intent, who knows what kind of trouble I could have caused? As it was, we had all gone through a rigorous screening process to even be approved for the meeting. "What is the name of your escort?" they demanded. "I don't know," I lied. I feared the young woman, a former White House intern, would be reprimanded, or fired. I also feared my walkabout might cause a problem for the RTNDA, resulting in another thirty-plus-year wait before the next sit-down with the president. I don't think either happened.

I wouldn't say they frogmarched me off the grounds. But it was close. I was ushered out onto Pennsylvania Avenue, escorted by a burly, square-jawed agent in a crisp uniform. I can only guess my name is now on a list somewhere, though given the recent state of security at the First Family's home, maybe not. Considering the recent challenges facing the Secret Service's White House detail, I am probably long forgotten.

When I got to CNN, I was dying to share the story of my unauthorized tour via satellite, with anchor Erick Thompson (who was filling in for me back home) and our viewers, but I thought better of it. What I did do, I'm afraid, was gush about the experience of meeting the president, and how my opinion of George W. Bush had changed for the better. No harm in that, but I am afraid my journalistic impartiality appeared in short supply. And I heard from viewers who were anti-Bush, who thought I had sold out. I won't re-litigate the decisions made in his presidency, from the Iraq War to Hurricane Katrina. But I will tell you that I liked him that day and gained a new respect.

I didn't get to ask my question, but in the end it didn't matter. I'd spent the afternoon in a meeting with a sitting president and had gone on a self-guided tour of the White House. Not a bad day.

The White House visit was not my only presidential close encounter. The following year, in 2006, I was invited to emcee an appearance in Victoria by former President Bill Clinton. He was on a speaking swing to British Columbia, with an afternoon speech at Victoria's Save-On-Foods Memorial Arena, followed by a similar address in Kelowna that night.

He was here on behalf of his Clinton Foundation, and would be discussing Canada–US relations. The $175-a-seat speech was a sellout. Clinton flew in after an appearance in New York the night before, with a stop in Washington, DC, on his way out west. His motorcade arrived slightly late, due in part to a fall downpour that afternoon. The rain also delayed the start of the event, with the thousands of people lined up outside getting soaked.

A VIP reception backstage was filled with a who's who of Victoria's business, political and philanthropic community. The format was simple. I would greet the audience, lay out the agenda, introduce a representative of CIBC, which was the title sponsor, thank the president, and then introduce Premier Gordon Campbell, who would lead a question-and-answer session. When that was over, I would return to the stage to thank them both and wrap it up.

When Bill Clinton walked into the reception, he lit up the room. For some reason I had expected to be indifferent, but I couldn't help but be charmed. There is no disputing the Clinton Charisma. But up close, he looked tired.

Time was tight, so after a few pleasantries and remarks, the guests lined up for a photo opportunity with Clinton. It was the day before Remembrance Day, so before the pictures, his handlers quickly pinned him with a poppy. Guests were ushered to their seats, and Clinton, Campbell and I were escorted backstage. But once behind the curtain, we were put on hold. Because of the rain, many of the seats were still empty; the people who'd paid for them were still lined up, still making their way in out of the rain.

Like many speakers, Clinton worked to keep his mind nimble before going on. And the wait seemed interminable. There we were, the former president, the premier and me, in a draped area the size of a closet, making small talk. We talked about golf, his previous visits to British Columbia, including a long-ago family visit with Hillary and Chelsea, Hillary's presidential aspirations, my recent White House visit and, inevitably, the weather.

Finally, the moment arrived. I was cued to take the podium, and the program was underway. I was especially proud to know that out there, in the sold-out arena, were Patty and her dad. Ron was a wonderful man who took great pride in our accomplishments, and I know it was a thrill for him (and Patty) to be there.

While Clinton spoke, the premier and I watched from back-stage, and I was flattered that he asked what questions I might ask if I were conducting the Q and A. I had several to offer, including something on strained relations, dusting off my old unanswered question from the White House.

Before we knew it, it was over, and we reconvened backstage. Clinton seemed happy. He had electrified the audience, delivered his message and pushed the work being done by his foundation. But the long hours suddenly showed. The bags under his eyes, which I had noticed beforehand, were bigger and darker now. He looked like he could use a nap. But his day wasn't over. Within minutes, he was on his way back to the airport and on to Kelowna.

As we chatted before he left, Clinton remarked that he liked my tie. And I appreciated the compliment for more than the obvious reason. The tie I had chosen for the day was lovely: silk, in a solid colour, which I had picked especially for him. It was bright blue, the closest shade I could find to the notoriously stained blue Gap dress made famous by Monica Lewinsky. I told no one, and no one but me knew the significance of it. A private joke for myself—no disrespect intended, Mr. President.

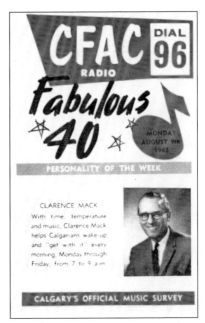

*The "Golden Age" of radio: my dad, Clarence Mack, at the mic at CFAC, circa 1950.*

*Clarence's* Toast and Marmalade *show was on top of the ratings in 1965.*

*Clarence produces a radio drama in the studio. CFAC News Director Don McDermid cues a record in the foreground.*

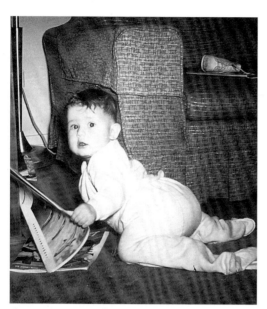

*Once a newsman, always a newsman. I was scanning the headlines as early as 1960.*

*Big Man on Campus: I graduated from Salmon Arm Senior High in '77.*

*My sister, Leilani, was the picture of courage and grace.*

*My mom and I have high tea at the Empress shortly after my arrival in Victoria in 1985.*

The brother I never knew, Darrel, with his dog, Laddie, in the early 1950s.

RTNDA Canada introduced the Byron MacGregor Award for best radio newscast in 1995 following Byron's death. His wife, Jo-Jo Shutty-MacGregor, seen here with KHJ Fredericton News Director Randy McKeen, presented the inaugural awards.

BYRON McGREGOR
GETTING YOU INTO THE NEWS
MORNINGS ON THE BIG 8!

My brother Gary, a.k.a. Byron MacGregor, on the cover of the CKLW Big 30. The record chart told me and every radio station in the world which songs to play every week.

Gary and me on one of my visits to Detroit in the late '70s.

*On a most memorable day in 2005, my RTNDA colleagues and I met with President George W. Bush at the White House. That's me, third from the right in the back row.*

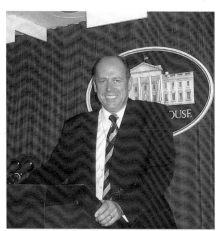

*Here I'm taking the podium in the White House Briefing Room. This was just before my unauthorized walkabout that had the Secret Service flipping out.*

*Another brush with the Oval Office. I hosted President Bill Clinton when he spoke in Victoria in 2006, wondering if he'd notice my tie.*

*The CTV news desk in the open concept studio/newsroom/control room was a great broadcasting environment.*
Photo courtesy Ilya Stavitsky

*One of the best pieces of promotional swag ever, the Hudson Mack lunch box became something of a collector's item.*

*Lloyd Robertson (left) and Craig Oliver (right) are news heroes and two real icons of Canadian journalism that I am proud to call friends. We're at a celebration of CTV News President Robert Hurst on his retirement.*

Two of my favourite charities are the Victoria Hospitals Foundation and Variety. I'm proud to have been part of the success of the VHF and the Variety Show of Hearts, and especially enjoyed supporting Jeneece Edroff's amazing fundraising.

The highlight of my community service so far was the 2009 Canadian Cancer Society Cops for Cancer Tour de Rock. With a lot of help, I set an individual record and raised more than $146,000 for children fighting cancer. We also rode our bikes more than a thousand kilometres.

The Tour de Rock was born out of the success of head shaves the year before. My CHEK colleague and good friend Alex Robertson helped get the ball rolling when we shaved our heads live on the air.

*Whether making toast for hungry students, reading to classes to support literacy programs, or here, working with BC Children's Hospital on the Miracle Network Telethon, I'll do anything I can to help kids.*

*Supporting our men and women in uniform in the Canadian Forces was an especially proud moment for me. I served as Honorary Lieutenant-Colonel for the 741 Communications Squadron in Victoria.*

The love of my life, Patty, and I married on the lawn of the Deep Cove Chalet on a hot September afternoon in 1988.

My dear niece Christy died unexpectedly at age thirteen on the day of my dad's birthday in 1995. We lost her just weeks after my brother's death. It was a terrible year.

There is nothing more precious to me than my family and time spent together. Here's me with Patty, Sheldon, Hamilton and Rachel on Willows Beach at the Oak Bay Tea Party.

Another beautiful day with the kids on another beautiful beach, this time in Maui in 2013 after renewing our wedding vows on our 25th anniversary.

# 15

# Famous People News

I t's not as though every day working in news involves meeting a monarch or a US president. But this career has made it possible for me to meet many prominent people, big names and stars. Some encounters have been all part of a day's work, but not all. I've never really been overly star-struck and for that reason am reluctant to list off the names of celebrities I've bumped into or interviewed, but there are a couple of stories worth retelling.

On July 11, 1989, Sir Laurence Olivier died. I never met him, but I knew there was a Hollywood biggie in Victoria that day that did know him, and even if he didn't know him well, it was a good enough reason to put him on TV.

A friend at the Empress Hotel had tipped me off that Bob Hope was in town. Hope was a regular visitor, and when he was in Victoria, he would usually play golf with the late Gorde Hunter, who was a local newspaper columnist. They'd play at the Victoria Golf Club in Oak Bay.

I knew my source wasn't supposed to tell me stuff like this, and I knew the hotel wouldn't confirm he was there. But I called on spec and asked to leave a message for Bob Hope. I figured it was worth a shot in the dark. About an hour later, I came back to the newsroom after leaving to work on something else, and reporter Patty Pitts had taken a message (remember, this is pre-voicemail days).

"Hey, one of your smartass friends called and left a message from Bob Hope."

I couldn't believe my ears. "What? What did he say? What did you say?"

"I told him to quit screwing around and tell who's really calling," Patty said, the cynical reporter in her refusing to believe it was really him.

I called back and left a second message, and wouldn't you know he called right back. He had heard about Olivier and would talk to us, but he wouldn't interrupt his golf game. If we wanted to talk, he'd give us five minutes on the first tee box—but the Hunter foursome was teeing off in twenty minutes.

Cameraman Garry Frang and I raced to the Victoria Club, which isn't easy. Racing through Oak Bay is a near impossibility—something that requires a great deal of patience. But we made it in time and I got to interview Bob Hope.

I found the tape years later. I look like I'm about ten years old, and my voice is high and squeaky; I was obviously nervous to be sitting down with this show biz legend. And he couldn't have been nicer. I'm still not sure if Patty Pitts ever believed it really was Bob Hope calling me back.

My Patty and I have always been big fans of the British soap opera *Coronation Street*. I can't remember exactly when we started watching it. I think her mom watched it years ago after coming to Canada from England, so Patty remembers the old black-and-white Ena Sharples era. I came into it later via my mom and sister who watched. But before long, Patty and I were hooked.

So we didn't think twice when we saw that two of the stars

of the show were going to be in Victoria on a publicity tour, promoting Royal Doulton china. Sue Nicholls, who for years has played the role of Audrey Roberts, and her real-life husband, Mark Eden, who used to play the villain Alan Bradley, were going to appear in the china department at The Bay department store downtown. They'd take photographs with fans and autograph a special commemorative *Coronation Street* plate. And we weren't going to miss it.

We showed up after the newscast early one evening, with toddler Rachel in tow; she ran wild in the china department while we lined up to meet the stars. We were the last ones in line, and when it was our turn, the local *Coronation Street* fan club rep introduced us, and explained I was the man from the local TV news. Someone offered to take a picture.

While we waited for the flash on the camera, Sue was giving me a big hug, worthy of her flirtatious Corrie character. Finally, we got the picture and the autographed plate or saucer and we were on our way before Rachel smashed anything.

Someone fed the story of this encounter to Jim Gibson, the local gossip columnist. He wrote it up in rather entertaining style, and I sent a clipping of the column and a copy of the picture to Sue and Mark. From that blossomed a great friendship that has endured over the years. And when we were passing through Heathrow Airport on one of our cruise escort trips, they insisted on hosting us in Manchester and giving us a private tour of the Grenada Studios where the series is produced.

We arrived in London in the morning, on our way home from the Mediterranean, and were greeted like visiting dignitaries. They could not have been nicer or more welcoming. Not only did we get to see behind the scenes and meet the entire cast, at least those involved in that day's shooting, we had lunch with them on the lot.

There's a thin line between fact and fiction, and the Old Schoolhouse Pub on the Granada Lot is an awful lot like The

Rover's Return. The pub was filled with familiar faces having a real pint and a hotpot before shooting resumed in the afternoon.

. Sue was so kind and genuinely interested in us and what we were doing. Mark was telling us stories of life after the *Street*. His character had recently been written out, killed off in Blackpool. Alan was hit by a streetcar while terrorizing Rita. Mark is a renowned playwright, but he described how his meetings with producers in London's West End would invariably drift to the goings-on in Weatherfield.

We have stayed in touch, and I was able to introduce them to another *Coronation Street* fan, my old arts reporter colleague Adam Sawatsky and his wife, Cheryl Bloxham, who also visited while in England.

Sue and Mark gave us a lovely commemorative book at the end of our visit and gave us a ride to the train. It was a remarkable day and the experience of a lifetime for anyone who is a fan of this great show.

It might not count as the biggest celebrity encounter, but it led to one of the coolest experiences we've had, and I'm still not sure how we pulled it off. Patty and I were in Los Angeles in October 2011 for an event she'd been invited to by Malibu realtor Madison Hildebrand. He's a bit of a celeb in his own right. And she'd introduced herself to him the previous summer at the Malibu Inn while we were having lunch on that San Francisco to LA holiday.

Madison invited us to a showing of a home in the hills overlooking Malibu and one of the canyons, which was being shot as part of his *Million Dollar Listing Los Angeles* program. I had surprised Patty by booking a bungalow at the Beverly Hills Hotel, where we'd spent the first few nights of our honeymoon.

There's always pretty good star gazing at the hotel, especially around the pool or in the Polo Lounge. And we could tell on the Saturday afternoon that something big was happening. It turns out it was the KISS wedding, Gene Simmons marrying Shannon Tweed, in the hotel that night.

We went to the Malibu showing, which was kind of fun, but didn't stay too late. There was a glimpse of us when the episode finally made it to air. Once we got back to the hotel, we went for a drink and something to eat in the Polo Lounge, where we chatted with Latoya Jackson, who was having dinner with her bodyguard. But the real action was happening in the hotel ballroom downstairs, where a who's who was celebrating the nuptials of Gene and Shannon.

On a flyer, I walked down to the end of the hotel corridor leading to the big curved staircase and gave my name to the security man at the desk. He looked through the list, but before he could find that our names were not there, I told him they weren't. But I explained who we were, and that we were Canadian like Shannon and her family, and that I was sure they'd be glad to see us. That's really all I told him. He said his boss would have to approve it, so he called him on his earpiece and the senior security man showed up. I laid it out a second time with no BS, and he said, "Yeah, I'm sure they'd be glad to have you join them." And with that, we were guests at the KISS wedding.

When we got to the ballroom, the reception was already underway. The room was beautiful, there was music and dancing and people were still eating dessert. We chatted with Gene and Shannon and their kids, Nick and Sophie. Shannon's sister hugged Patty like a long-lost friend. (People always seem to think they've met Patty before or should know her.)

We fit right in, and hung out for a while with Dog the Bounty Hunter and his wife, Beth. There were plenty of people in the room we didn't recognize, probably music industry types. But we didn't try to scam our way in and we didn't lie about who we were or why we were there. And we stayed a long time, almost to the end, and felt welcome throughout.

The whole thing was being shot for Gene and Shannon's

reality show, *Gene Simmons Family Jewels*, but like the Malibu open house, our appearance was fleeting. There was a pretty good shot of Patty on the dance floor, but that was about it. A great night to celebrate with a big-name couple who are really down to earth and nice, normal folks.

Hollywood and Beverly Hills are, of course, the place to be for this kind of thing. And once, on a previous trip, we bumped into Liza Minnelli on Rodeo Drive. She and a friend were buying shoes. She looked like anybody else out shopping that day—that is to say, anyone shopping where the shoes start at twenty-five hundred bucks a pair.

I didn't want to bug her, but she was happy to meet me, and she agreed to take a photo. I guess paparazzi has changed that, and the fact that everyone everywhere now carries a camera in their phone and can make money selling embarrassing pictures to the likes of TMZ has also made people in the public eye a little more leery of people like me coming up with my little camera.

This past summer we bumped into Conan O'Brien having lunch in Malibu. He couldn't have been nicer, especially to our kids, and made sure we all got to attend his show the next day, even hanging out in the Green Room.

Everything is relative, and in a small way, it makes me understand better why people might be excited to meet me in public, after inviting me into their homes each night for so long. That's why I always have tried to be kind and polite, even if the timing or circumstances weren't the best. People are mostly polite and don't want to intrude. Mostly. I don't include the old woman in the grocery store who poked me in the belly like the Pillsbury Doughboy. Or that drunk logger in the pub at the Columbus Hotel in Prince George.

If members of the public are impressed to meet people in our business, so too are people in our business, myself included. During my years on the RTNDA boards in Canada and the United

States, I've had a chance to meet many of the luminaries of our industry, and I was impressed by nearly every one of them.

I have always had an enormous respect for Dan Rather, and will always be glad to have made Dan's acquaintance and to be able to call him a friend. I was honoured that he was willing to speak on my RTNDA President's Award tribute video and to say such nice things. Dan, I might take you up on that offer of bail money someday!

The video also featured many of the giants of broadcast journalism in Canada, including Lloyd Robertson and Craig Oliver. Lloyd and I have been friends for many years, and I had the honour of hosting an intimate question period with him during his book tour a few years ago. Craig and I go back as well. We share an email incident that taught me to make sure I was hitting "forward" and not "reply," in which I inadvertently called him an "asshole." We laugh about it now.

I was disappointed to meet Walter Cronkite. I don't know if he was having a bad day, but I was left with a bad impression of a cranky curmudgeon who couldn't even feign some charm for several of us who could barely contain our glee at meeting this news icon.

Oprah Winfrey's handlers stopped me from taking a picture of her eating during an RTNDA luncheon once. They might have a harder time stopping that now, in the smart-phone era. I guess I don't blame her, but I've never taken myself that seriously.

Charles Osgood, Koppel and Brokaw, and a young Katie Couric—these are just a few of the people in our industry that I've met thanks to the RTDNA. And they all have something in common, which I share too: a love of our business and the good things it can do.

# 16

## The Big Story

I am often asked what I think is the most memorable story of my career, or the interview I'll never forget. It's a hard question to answer, because over a span of thirty-five years on the air, there are just too many to list. From tragedies to triumphs, there are the news days you'll always remember and others that were spent in search of a lead story.

It's a cliché to say that those of us in the news industry have a front seat to history, but it's true. We have traditionally been the first to find out about something. But not always.

December 8, 1980, was one of those nights. I had been at CFJC radio and television in Kamloops for just a few months; it was my first full-time job in the business, and I was still green as grass.

The old layout of the Kamloops station had the newsroom in the middle of the building—radio at one end and television at the other. But getting to the TV area meant going down the hall into a separate room.

We were a CBC affiliate at the time, and though we didn't carry the CBC Vancouver suppertime newscast, we recorded it and stripped provincial stories from the tape to play back on our late show. After I read my hourly radio cast at seven o'clock, I stapled and filed the copy and laid out a barebones framework for the following hour. Then I went down the hall to dub off the CBC stories and transcribe intros and other information from the Vancouver cast, which was anchored at the time by Bill Good (still known then as Bill Good, Jr.) and Cecelia Walters.

I was young, keen and earnest and was working away for most of the hour without going back into the radio area to check the Broadcast News wire service. In those days, there were no computers in the newsroom—everything was on paper, story after story moving over the wire, rolling up and over the back of the wire machine, which clattered away incessantly. The wire would also ding an alarm bell for an urgent piece of copy. Three dings was a big deal. However, for nearly an entire hour, I was out of the room and didn't hear a thing.

So a few minutes before eight o'clock, I was ripping copy off the wire, pulling the hockey score summary to set aside for the two jocks who were on the air on our AM and FM stations (still staffed with warm bodies and not automation in those days). I was discarding the copy we didn't need and pulling the stories I'd use in the newscast that was coming up in the next few minutes.

As we ripped copy from the roll of paper spilling down the back of the wire machine, we worked backwards in time—the most recently moved items, of course, were first as you scrolled through. I noticed there seemed to have been a lot of material moving in that hour, and I soon discovered why.

URGENT—John Lennon killed by assassin, more to follow. FLASH—Lennon dead. BULLETIN—Reports of John Lennon shot outside New York City apartment.

And on and on it went, as I read in horror, working my way back in time through the first reports of his murder—which had moved much earlier in the hour, just minutes after I had gone down the hall to cannibalize the CBC Evening News.

There was just enough time before the top of the hour to pull off a voice report from the audio feed, a breathless account of the tragedy from a reporter on the sidewalk outside the Dakota Apartments. I got the newscast on the air and reported the assassination of Beatle John Lennon. It was nearly an hour after the news had broken.

I was shattered. And stunned, of course, by the news itself. I felt sick that my first big story—BIG STORY—even if it was from far away and delivered over the wire, I had mishandled so badly. The two jocks were fuming that we were so late on it. Usually, they were in and out of the newsroom several times in the hour, checking the wire for sports scores—but not that night.

It only got worse when I learned later that Howard Cosell had broken the news to millions during the broadcast of Monday Night Football. I had turned the game off in the TV area. I didn't want to be distracted, so earnest was I. And to add insult to injury, we later learned that our cross-town radio competition, CHNL, had had the story on the air from the first bulletin shortly after seven o'clock and had been playing Lennon and Beatles music non-stop since. Could it be any worse? CHNL did not even have an evening newscaster on shift. The jock, Glen McIntyre (who later became a friend), had heard their BN wire dinging madly and checked to see what was happening. It did little to comfort me that their studio and newsroom were separated only by an open sliding glass door, not a long way down the hall.

I felt sick for the rest of the night. After the late TV cast, we licked our wounds over cold beers across the street from the station at the Dome Motor Inn. Many hours were spent in there, overlooking CFJC and the twinkling lights of Kamloops below. But on this night, the lights didn't seem very bright.

John Lennon was dead. And I had missed it.

Reluctant as I am to fill these pages with regrets of the stories I have missed, I am compelled to also share the tale of the October

1989 Loma Prieta earthquake that hit San Francisco and the Bay Area. These recollections are fresh, because the twenty-fifth anniversary of the quake just happened, and I was able to relive the day with my cohort Alex Robertson, who was also there.

We were both working at CHEK TV at the time, and the station was then a CTV network affiliate. As such, it was carrying the ABC TV feed of the World Series, which was unusual that year, in that it pitted the San Francisco Giants against their Across-The-Bay American League rivals, the Oakland Athletics. The pre-game coverage began at 5:00 PM our time, with the first pitch around 5:25. This pre-empted our usual 5:30 local newscast, so we aired the broadcast an hour early at 4:30. For some reason, perhaps due to the imminent demise of our news director of the day, our general manager, Jim Nicholl, was unusually interested in the workings of the newsroom. He had dropped down in the afternoon to make sure we had assembled a backup broadcast that we could rush to air at 5:30 in the event of a rainout.

We did duplicate a few scripts and re-cue some of the stories that had run at 4:30, but none of us was too keen to stick around in the unlikely event of a rainout or postponement of the game. All afternoon we checked the newswire for the current weather from San Francisco. This was before the internet, so information like this was not at everyone's fingertips. It could not have been a better day by The Bay. It was sunny and crisp, without a hint of rain of wind, promising a glorious evening for game three of the fall classic. With no rainout in the works, Alex remarked, "The only thing that will postpone this game is an earthquake!" We have since marvelled at the prescience of this offhand remark at the lineup table.

We aired the 4:30 newscast live, signed off and checked the weather one more time. The ABC feed was on the air, the coverage revealing what we knew from the wire—great weather and nothing amiss. So, with that, we bolted for the door to get away early for a change. It was barely 5:01.

This is where recollections get fuzzy. Alex insists we had a tee time at the Gorge Vale Golf Course, and I think we might have, but I know we didn't go golfing. I had just completed a renovation of my Mustang, which was in need of upholstery, paint and body work after its duty as a "daily driver" in Prince George. It was fresh out of the shop, with a gleaming new white convertible top and a coat of red paint that would put a fire engine to shame.

On my way home, I stopped near our home at the summit of Mount Tolmie, a regional park with enough elevation to give you a spectacular view of Greater Victoria, the Juan de Fuca Strait and the mountains on Washington's Olympic Peninsula. I parked the Mustang in several places to capture each backdrop and took pictures of my "new" old car.

When I got home, it was a little after 5:30, and since I can never watch my competitors while I am on the air myself, I turned on the TV to see the CKVU (then known as U.TV) newscast, anchored by Russ Froese. I cannot describe the pit I felt in my stomach as I watched and heard him narrate the early scenes of destruction from San Francisco.

At 5:04 PM, a time-stamp that would ring in my ears all night, as it was repeated on the coverage, a massive earthquake had hit San Francisco. Measuring 6.9 in magnitude, it killed sixty-three people and did major damage, leaving freeways pancaked, sections of bridges collapsed, buildings crumbled and burned. The world, at least the world watching baseball, was made aware of the quake as it happened. ABC sports broadcaster Al Michaels was interrupted mid-sentence by the shaking. Shortly after that, the feed from Candlestick Park was lost and broadcasters were on their own for coverage. This was still early days for all-news cable networks, which today would have been wall-to-wall with breaking news coverage, complete with graphics giving the disaster a dramatic name, and a soundtrack of sad-sounding cellos.

I switched over to Channel 6, dreading what I would find. There, in my anchor chair, was Lee Mackenzie, who was then our late anchor, doing her best to stickhandle the story live on the air, while weaving in with some of the local stories and regurgitated content we had left behind from the 4:30 broadcast.

I ran from our house, jumped back into the freshly restored and repainted Mustang and drove like a maniac to the station, a trip that would normally have taken about ten or fifteen minutes, but not now with traffic. Just a couple of blocks from the studio, I nearly crashed into a truck that suddenly turned left in front of me. I came inches from totalling my beautiful car, one day after getting it restored. The scare in the intersection smartened me up. I drove like a normal person for the last block or so. I knew it was already too late. As I skulked into the newsroom and studio, the newscast limped along, the worst of the scramble over, and it was obvious there was nothing I could do to help at that point.

That night at home, we watched the quake coverage, which seemed be punctuated by the incessant on-air references to the time it hit, "5:04, 5:04 . . ." The time-stamp plunged like a dagger every time. In the end, Alex was right; it took an earthquake to stop that game.

When I am asked what I consider my greatest story or accomplishment in news, it's hard to nail down. Like anyone who was on the air on September 11, 2001, that day will stand out like no other. I will always be proud of the work we did that day, locally and as part of the national network coverage.

Rob Germain was still on the assignment desk at CHEK on that terrible morning. He broke the news to me, calling my house just after 6:00 AM Pacific time, after the second hijacked plane hit the World Trade Centre. I couldn't believe what I was hearing on the phone until I turned on the TV and we watched together.

Like New York, Victoria woke up to a beautiful September morning, without a cloud in the sky. I was in the Mustang with the roof down, listening to news on the AM radio. Every station was carrying the audio from a network TV feed, mostly

CNN. I remember the sound was even more horrific without the pictures.

We had a quick meeting in the newsroom before my cameraman and I set out to find local reaction and Americans trying to get home. We found people in tears in the lobby of the Fairmont Empress, US citizens checking out as fast as they could, not knowing yet there'd be no more flights that day. We went to the lineup for the morning sailing of the Coho ferry to Port Angeles. Stunned looks of disbelief, some anger, more tears. We were invited by a California couple onboard their beautiful motor-home, to watch the unbelievable pictures coming from New York, and then Washington.

Interestingly, the Coho terminal in Victoria had played a role in thwarting a terrorist attack less than two years earlier. The so-called Millennium Bomber, Ahmed Rassam, was apprehended in Port Angeles as he drove off the Coho ferry. American border agents had been tipped off by their Canadian colleagues in Victoria to check a suspicious passenger and vehicle. They found a trunkful of explosives he intended to use to bomb the Los Angeles airport, LAX, to mark the arrival of 2000.

At the front of the California couple's luxury coach was a big flat-screen TV over the windshield, and on it was Peter Jennings of ABC News, narrating the unimaginable scene as the South Tower at the World Trade Centre collapsed first. The look on the couple's faces defies description. I looked out the side window over Victoria's beautiful inner harbour, without as much as a ripple on the water, under a brilliant blue morning sky. It didn't seem real, that at that very moment such horror was unfolding in lower Manhattan.

It was a day that went by quickly but seemed to take forever. I was back in the studio doing local segments into the national feed, getting as much local information and reaction as we could. We did a good job that day, ourselves and as an industry, informing and assuring as best we could, in the face of a despicable attack that would change the world forever.

A tragedy on the waters of Elk Lake, north of Victoria, will also always stand out in my memory. Two rowers from the University of Victoria died on January 15, 1988, when a sudden windstorm hit the lake while they were training on the water. Elk Lake is the training site for the UVic rowing team, and it has since become the headquarters for the national rowing program.

On this winter day, there were two UVic men's novice eights, one coach and one launch on the water. It was late in the afternoon, and a rapidly moving frontal system cut across Vancouver Island, with some of the highest winds recorded for that time of year, sudden gusts as high as eighty kilometres an hour. Near the north end of the lake, at the farthest point from the boathouse, were the rowing sculls. Both of the eights swamped. The launch, or training boat that follows along, was able to get half of the rowers out of the icy water, but it swamped before it could get to shore. It was getting darker and the wind was getting stronger, and it was an hour before rescuers found the second eight. By then, one of the rowers had drowned, and a second died from hypothermia.

This all began to happen while I was sitting at the CHEK assignment desk, as our 5:30 newscast, anchored by Mark Jan Vrem, was on the air. The emergency calls on the police and fire scanner were frantic. I called cameraman Rob Simpson and we raced to the lake, which was about twenty minutes away.

By the time we got there, the wind was howling, emergency crews were scrambling and it was dark. Everyone knew there were rowers in the water, but rescuers couldn't find them. We waited at the boathouse for an Armed Forces Chinook helicopter to arrive from 442 Squadron in Comox. It seemed to take forever.

You could hear it coming, long before the chopper came into sight. And when it did, it was an eerie thing to behold, coming over the horizon, the blinding beam of its searchlight criss-crossing the choppy water below.

In terms of newsgathering technology, these were the old days. The station had just taken delivery of new Betacam ENG units, and

I remember Rob tripping in the dark over a low concrete wall. He was able to twist and save the camera but hurt his shoulder. There were no cellphones; we relied on two-way radios in the news vans. But I was able to find a landline telephone in time to call in a quick hit to the BCTV News Hour, which was still on the air until seven o'clock.

We packaged the story for our late news and the network at eleven: the search, the recovery, the survivors' stories, the family members and teammates waiting on shore. Later, we would cover the investigation and the changes in safety policy for the rowing program that were the result.

My story that night won an RTNDA award for CHEK, for "Best Breaking News." Winning awards for someone else's heartbreak never feels right, but that's part of what we do, and I was proud of our work. But what I will always remember most about that night was the seemingly endless wait in the dark with the others, helplessly knowing somebody's son or brother was out there in that icy water. I will never forget the haunting sound of the approaching rescue chopper and the sight of its searchlight, at last.

# 17

# What's in a Name?

There has always been something about names in my family. We've either wished we were called something else, called ourselves something else or liked what we're called just fine. I fall into that third category.

Hudson Mack sounds like one of those made-up names that broadcasters used to choose when an air name was common. But it's the real thing, and there's a story behind it.

After Darrel died and my sister Leilani was born, my parents and their young family were on a motor trip across Canada. They drove from Calgary to southern Ontario, where they were going to visit my uncle Bud and his wife and family in the town of Ancaster. They were driving a Hudson Jet, or maybe it was a Wasp. Anyway, the car was a Hudson. And not far from Ancaster, just outside Hamilton, Ontario, the rear axle split and the car wouldn't move. So they hunkered down in Hamilton for a couple of nights and waited for the Hudson to get fixed. This, apparently, is where the miracle of conception occurred.

As the story has been retold over the years, it has been

embellished, to my mom's everlasting horror. *Times Colonist* gossip columnist Jim Gibson got wind of it. His version of the story had the conception occurring in the backseat of the Hudson. That's not what happened. My mother was aghast. Sorry, Mom.

When family friend Dr. Harry Oborne, the obstetrician who delivered me in 1960, put the timeline together, it was clear to him that I should be called Hudson Hamilton Mack—named for a broken-down car in the city where it all started. My parents had apparently thought of calling me Philip. But the more my folks thought about Hudson, the better they liked it, and here I am.

It was kind of a big name for a little kid. It does sound like a dreamed-up stage name, and all my life people have thought it should be Mack Hudson, the other way around, which I suppose makes sense. If I am ever checking into a hotel and they have no record of the reservation, I always get them to check Mack Hudson, and that's how they usually have me listed. For the longest time, I'd never heard of anyone else called Hudson, but it has become more common as a first name. And when I see the birth announcements around here that herald the arrival of little Hudsons, I like to think it may be the result of my influence after being on the air here for so long, but that's just me.

A lifetime later, when our first son was born, Patty suggested taking my middle name for him. And Hamilton is a great name that really suits him. He's Ham or Hammy to his friends and family, just as I am Hud or Huddy to mine. Hammy loves his name.

My dad never really liked the name Clarence. I'm not really sure how his parents came to make that choice in 1920, though I think it was more common then. There weren't a lot of Clarences around, though, other than *Clarence, the Cross-eyed Lion* from the 1965 movie. And of course there is Clarence, the angel who saves George Bailey in *It's a Wonderful Life*. He always makes me think of my dad when we watch that holiday favourite every Christmas.

Clarence's nickname in the old radio days was "Cy," though I am not sure why. It's not a usual abbreviation, and there was actually another broadcaster called Cy Mack in Ontario around the same time. My dad used to always say he wished he'd been called Sheldon, which is the name of our youngest son.

It was Patty's suggestion that we call him Sheldon. I didn't know until later that my mom had shared that information with her. I think Sheldon is a great name and it really suits my son. He sometimes muses that it wouldn't have been his first choice, but I think he likes it, and I think it's a great name.

Our daughter, Rachel, makes noises sometimes about wishing she had been called something else, but I think she likes it. We made the mistake of telling her once that we considered calling her Georgia, which would also have been a good choice. I think what stopped us was my fear of a lifetime of listening to Patty put on a southern accent to talk about our "L'il Georgia Peach."

Folks who don't know us might assume we are Jewish, with two of our children named Rachel and Sheldon, both good historic Hebrew handles. Sheldon was originally a surname derived from a place name, meaning "valley with steep sides." Rachel was the second and favoured wife of Jacob in the Old Testament, and the name means "little lamb." She is certainly that.

My mom was never crazy about her name, Murdena. It was a hybrid of her parents' names, Murdoch and Lachena McGregor. I always thought it was kind of cool, but it was one of these names people seem never know how to pronounce when they hit it.

And that's one of the reasons my sister sometimes wished she'd been named something else. Her name was inspired by my dad's love of Hawaii. At his urging, my parents named their daughter Leilani (Hawaiian for "heavenly flower"), most likely inspired by the Bing Crosby song "Sweet Leilani." I'm not sure if my mom was as keen about it as my dad was, but the Hawaiian name stuck (though it was actually her middle name—Cathrine being her first, also unusual with a missing e, as in my mother's middle name).

She'd cringe in a new classroom when the teacher was taking attendance. The long pause would always precede a couple of stabs at pronouncing her name. Among the many variants on her name over the years, my favourite came in 1967 on the train home from Montreal to Calgary, after our parents had taken us to Expo 67. A girl she'd made friends with on the train kept coming to the door asking for "Little Annie."

But when it comes to names, the real story in our family is my brother's, and it also happened in 1967. Gary Lachlan Mack became Byron MacGregor when he moved to Windsor to go to work at CKLW. It was commonplace at the time for on-air people to take on a different persona. In this case there were similarly named DJs at the station, Billy Mack and Gary something. So adding a newsman named Gary Mack was not going to work, and news director Dick Smyth told my brother he'd have to call himself something else on the air.

"A different name?" my brother asked. "Like what?"

"Do you have any relatives whose name you like?" Smyth replied.

Gary explained that he was staying at his uncle's until he got settled. "His name is Byron MacGregor," he told him.

"Byron MacGregor?" Smyth bellowed. "That's a great name. You'll be Byron MacGregor!"

The original Byron, our uncle Bud, was living in the Detroit suburb of Royal Oak, working as a commercial artist in the auto industry. That's who Gary was staying with. When he went home that night to ask, Bud wasn't initially very keen.

Byron MacGregor wasn't really Bud's original name either. He was born Alexander Bell McGregor (Bell was Lachena's maiden name). But as an adult, he embraced the Kabalarian philosophy, in which each letter in your name has a value and you add the numbers to themselves to see what your destiny number is. I suspect this is an oversimplification of the Kabalarian way, but you get the idea. As it turned out, Alex, I mean Byron, I mean

Bud, didn't like the number, so he changed it. I assume it was the numeric value that inspired Uncle Bud to change the "Mc" in McGregor to "Mac," so my brother's was "Mac" too.

Bud may not have initially liked his nephew taking his adopted handle, but as Gary/Byron became increasingly well known and a media star in Detroit, he began to like it. Someone who did not, though, was Clarence. And when Gary became known internationally through "The Americans," I think it really hurt our dad. That added further strain to their relationship, I'm sure. And I can't help but think the dual identity must have been hard on Gary sometimes.

He never legally changed his name. His birth certificate and driver's licence always remained Gary Mack. But he was, and will always be, Byron to the people who knew and loved him in Windsor and Detroit. And I couldn't have loved and admired him more no matter what anyone called him.

One more story about names, this one involving Patty. When we were married in 1988, the ceremony was presided over by the late Father Leo Robert. He was the Catholic priest at Patty's parents' church, as well as the minister at the UVic multi-faith chapel. Father Leo was a cool guy and quite a character.

In the lead-up to the ceremony, Patty and I each had several meetings with him, and one day, in a roundabout way, he revealed that Patty was not planning to change her name after the wedding; she would continue to be known by her maiden name, Pat Moores. (She also had a name-related pet peeve, when people who called her "Patsy" as a child kept doing it into adulthood.)

I was a little miffed about the name thing at first, but Leo was able to talk me off the ledge and realize it wasn't a big deal. And since we were both still working at CHEK at the time, it didn't hurt to maintain separate identities, not that it really mattered.

For our tenth anniversary, Patty changed her name from Pat Moores to Patty Mack. By then I was indifferent but was glad once she did. It made sense then with the children being born. And she switched Pat to Patty. She assumes I'm in a snit if I refer to her as Pat, or bray it at her like an old boss used to. Maybe she switched to Patty because it scans better with Mack. "Nick knack, Patty Mack." It's actually a pretty good way to remember her name.

# 18

## Giving Back

I have always held that people in the public eye, especially broadcasters who have gained influence where they live, have a responsibility to use it for good. I hope that doesn't sound corny, because I believe it to be true. We have an obligation to use the profile that is on loan to us, to help others. And I stress *on loan*, because it isn't ours to keep. I have always tried to do that and I hope in some small way I have helped.

I am proud to have been able to take part in the Variety Show of Hearts Telethon while I was at CHEK. Participating in the annual broadcast, and supporting fundraisers throughout the year, has been a highlight for me. British Columbians are generous and they step up to help families whose children are often fighting for their lives.

It was indirectly through Variety that I became friends with Victoria's Jeneece Edroff. She is living with a condition called neurofibromatosis, which causes tumours to grow on nerve tissues. Jeneece has been a tireless supporter of Variety, and more recently through her own foundation, which created Jeneece Place, for families, at Victoria General Hospital. Jeneece is best known for her penny drive, which has raised well over a million dollars and counting, one penny at a time. When I was at CHEK, she asked me if I'd help. And it's one of the best things I've been able to do. But I didn't do anything, really. Jeneece did.

Speaking of Variety, I don't know where it is, but there is a Sunshine Coach somewhere on Vancouver Island with my name on it. A donation of $1,047 earns you recognition on one of the vans that Variety provides to help get children where they need to go. I received the Distinguished Service Award from the RTNDA several years ago, and Canada Newswire (as it was known then) made a thousand dollar donation to the charity of my choice, which it generously does for the recipient each year. I chose Variety and rounded it up to $1,047. My name and Canada Newswire's are on a Sunshine Coach, and that feels good.

I've also been a proud supporter of the Victoria Hospitals Foundation, expertly led by my friend Melanie Mahlman. For many years, I hosted the foundation's major fundraising effort, Visions. More recently, I have been honoured to support VHF in its ongoing campaigns, such as Building Care Together, to purchase much-needed hospital equipment.

I also believe in supporting the men and women of our military. And I was honoured to serve for several years as an Honourary Lieutenant-Colonel in the Canadian Forces, for the 741 Communications Squadron in Victoria. I will admit to feeling out of my depth at times, having had no military experience. But I now understand the pride one feels donning the uniform of his or her country, and I have even greater respect for our servicemen and women, and the sacrifices they and their families make.

Perhaps my greatest success in supporting a charitable cause has been my involvement with the Canadian Cancer Society, specifically the Cops for Cancer Tour de Rock. My involvement with Cops for Cancer predates the annual bike ride, where participants ride more than one thousand kilometres down the length of Vancouver Island, raising money and awareness for children's cancer programs, and funding Camp Goodtimes for youngsters fighting the disease.

It all started in Edmonton, where a police officer shaved his head to show solidarity with a child who was self-conscious when chemotherapy made his hair fall out. Soon head shaves were happening in other cities, too, including Victoria.

My friend and colleague Ed Bain, from The Q and CHEK (who, by the way, is one of the nicest and funniest people you'll ever meet), was presiding over a mass head shave at a downtown mall in Victoria, and we had run a short item on the news at CHEK, showing a couple of police officers being shaved in advance to promote the event. I quipped at the end of the newscast that I'd shave my head live on TV if we could raise enough money. My longtime colleague and good friend, sportscaster Alex Robertson, said he'd do it too.

By the time we got back to the newsroom, the phones were ringing off the hook: a hundred dollar pledge here, fifty there, another call promising five hundred dollars. So, after winning the approval of station management (and it took some arm twisting), we did it. The response was overwhelming, and the on-air push helped make the mass shave-in a huge success.

Organizers wanted to build on the momentum we had helped build, so they launched the Tour de Rock the following year. And every September since, a team of police officers and media riders get on their bikes and ride from the northern tip of Vancouver Island to Victoria, stopping in school gyms and community centres, raising money and accepting donations as they go.

CHEK became a media partner, though I never rode while I was there.

When I joined The New VI, I made the Tour de Rock a priority. Some people, including at least one of the ride organizers, thought I was trying to steal CHEK's thunder. Anything but. It is an event that galvanizes communities, brings people together in a common goal and helps children with cancer. Why would anyone not do everything they could to help?

Several years later, in the lead-up to the 2009 ride, the Cancer Society came to A-Channel, as we were known then, inviting us to be their media partner. Our answer was an enthusiastic yes. My opportunity to ride had arrived. And my timing was good. Throughout the previous fall, I had undertaken a very public campaign on-air to lose weight and get fit. We called it "The Mack Over" with Bala Fitness, and each week viewers could peek at the scale with me and see how my trainer, Melissa Clarke, was helping me get in better shape. I lost about fifty pounds by the time it was over. Had I not, the ride might have been even more of a challenge.

What many people don't know is that the thousand or more kilometres logged during the two-week ride is a fraction of the mileage you put on training for six months beforehand. And as the ride gets closer, there are fewer hours spent on the bike, and many more spent fundraising.

I had the good fortune of having a very good team behind me. Patty stepped up immediately and organized a committee of friends and volunteers to support my fundraising. A-Channel staff, especially Bruce Williams, worked hard too and organized and ran a number of events.

Philips Brewery bottled a special commemorative beer, "Hud Light," with partial proceeds going to the Tour. Peninsula Co-Op staged a summer-long gasoline-for-a-year raffle. There were leg waxings and fashion shows, car washes, and beer and burger nights. And with the generous support of Stormin' Norman Jackson at the Cowichan Golf and Country Club, we staged the first of many very lucrative Tour de Rock golf tournaments. That's just some of what we did. When the donations in my name were tallied, we had raised a record individual total, more than $146,000. So many people helped. I am so fortunate to have had such support. Thank you.

Cycling a thousand kilometres was surprisingly manageable, though we benefited from extremely good weather (except for a couple of days). The ride truly is an experience of a lifetime, and with only a couple of exceptions over the years, people only get to do it once. It is truly life-changing. The families you meet, the children, your honourary rider, a youngster fighting cancer, the kids at Camp Goodtimes. The cops. People you will never forget. Like the mother flipping burgers for us in the logging hamlet of Woss, with a population of two hundred. Her daughter was with her, and as we chatted, her cancer story came spilling out—not childhood cancer, but her mother's diagnosis. Telling me about it seemed to help, and as we pedalled up the hill and back to the highway, she was at the side of the road, mouthing "thank you" through her sobs.

One of the most precious gifts any of us can give is our time. Whether it is ringing bells beside a Salvation Army kettle, reading to children or seniors, or volunteering at a street shelter, there is always something we can do, if only we look.

I get my inspiration from many corners, and I especially admire people who have earned success in business, and give back. There is no better example of that on Vancouver Island than the Campbell family. The Thrifty Foods co-founder, the late Alex Campbell, his wife, Jo, and their children, Alex, Bonnie and Lorne, set the example.

I was humbled to be invited by the Campbell family to host the program at the memorial service celebrating Alex Campbell's life. An overflow crowd packed the Victoria Conference Centre to thank the man who "put smiles in the aisle" and did so much to help so many others. It was an honour I will always cherish. We should all be more like him.

Please don't think I am offering up a laundry list of good works in the name of self-aggrandizement. I am not and would not. I simply believe each of us has a responsibility to help, whether we are in the public eye or not. For those of us who have, or have had, the benefit of a public persona, it is a calling that must not be ignored.

# 19

# Brave New World

I get a little weary when I hear people bemoaning the state of the media, especially those who keep delivering the last rites for television. "I'm not dead yet," TV media would say, like the voice from the back of a wagon in a Monty Python movie. If only it could speak for itself.

Communication is evolving by the day, as it has since the days of paintings on cave walls. The changes are coming so fast that it's a revolution, not an evolution. How do you think storytelling started? Some caveman couldn't understand the picture and asked for an explanation. I'm sure the other caveman struggled to find the right word. But eventually he did, even if he had to create it. We are almost back to as primal a state today.

The blinding speed at which communication technology is advancing, and the ever-increasing wash of information that continuously soaks us, cannot help but make us a little antsy, worried that we're losing control. "We" being those who have been part of conventional media as we know it, who realize the control is long gone.

But a greater threat to things the way we have always known them is the way people consume media. The future is mobile and there is no looking back. I remember a presentation at that first RTNDA conference I attended in Whistler in 1990. Futurist Frank Ogden was talking about "News on Demand," people getting what news they wanted, where and when they wanted it. And nobody had ever thought of the term "citizen journalist" (which bugs me, by the way), or the concept, but even then Frank was musing about how the end user would become part of the process. Most of us thought it sounded pretty far-fetched. How little we knew.

The internet has killed a lot of industries so far. It hasn't killed television yet, but it is working on it. Yet TV will not disappear, just as the Gutenberg press has not, nor AM radio.

The issue for people who make their living from conventional media as we knew it—and the investors who make their dividends from it—is that the game has changed and will never be the same again. There is still money to be made, maybe not as much and maybe not the old way. And it isn't just the business model that's been turned upside down. The rise of new media has created new issues and questions of ethics.

In our country, one of the hurdles to overcome, maybe even as big as technological change, is the bureaucracy of regulation. The rules as they exist, written for a time long gone, cannot help but stifle the success and future of some segments of the media. If conventional television in Canada is on its deathbed, the CRTC just might be at its bedside, ready to hold a pillow over its face.

I have been part of this scene for close to thirty-five years, and I've seen a few changes myself. When I attended SAIT in 1978, we learned to physically splice tape with china markers and razor blades, because that was a skill still in demand. When I worked in Kamloops at my first real job in broadcasting, film cameras had only recently been phased out, but the new portable videotape technology, ENG, was still bulky and cumbersome. When I was on a reporter's beat in Prince George, I still carried alligator clips and scanned hotel lobbies for payphone locations while covering news conferences. I carried a film can full of quarters for those phones, to call and feed tape down the line for the top of the hour. I used to have a friend on the research desk at the library who would look stuff up for me when I needed some quick facts. When I got to CHEK, the mail (we'd never have thought to call it snail mail—was there any other kind?) was still relevant in the newsroom, and a news release sent a day earlier (or longer) would still get picked up. Then came the miracle of the fax machine.

Even the state-of-the-art technology like that which CHUM equipped The New VI with was obsolete in a few years. The server-based video systems and desktop editing are now the norm, and people can do essentially the same thing on their laptops at home, or more often than not, on their phones.

This might all sound like Old Fart Speak—"When I was a cub reporter . . ."—but the fact is, the industry, and the technology that drives it, is always changing and always will be. Like most things, it all boils down to money.

In the 2000s, in the midst of the "Fee for Carriage" fights between the broadcasters and what they call the BDUs (Broadcast Distribution Units), cable or satellite companies, the CRTC kicked the can down the road, hoping to buy time. And what many in the industry, including me, predicted at the time, has come to pass. The BDUs simply bought out the broadcasters. If you are going to have to pay them for their signals, eat them first, so you're just moving money from one pocket to the other.

Look at what's happened. Shaw Media picked up the pieces, at least the broadcast ones, after CanWest Global went bankrupt. Bell Media swallowed up CTV. And Rogers already ran its own broadcast division.

Oh yeah, there's also the CBC. It feels it should also be protected against the BDUs, but it gets about a billion dollars a year from the likes of you and me, so that should help. But I am not anti-CBC, despite years of newsroom ranting. A healthy public broadcaster is important to a country, and in the CBC we have a very good one. My issue is that it wants the best of both worlds: cashing that big cheque from Ottawa each year, while also competing with the private broadcasters for scarce advertising dollars.

For broadcasters, the sky was falling. "Save Local TV," we cried, in ad campaigns, street rallies and letter writing campaigns. I can't count how many times we solicited letters of support from the same people, asking them to say the same things to the same politicians. And did viewers ever really understand, or care? Their main concern has always been how much they have to pay to keep getting what they want. And the cable and satellite companies made it clear that if they have to pay, customers will have to pay, and you can blame your local TV station for that.

In a typically Canadian solution (why did the chicken walk to the middle of the road?), the CRTC's answer was a compromise on Fee for Carriage, the money broadcasters say cable companies should pay for local signals. Instead of mandating that the cable companies have to find a solution and work with the broadcasters to do it, the commission introduced the LPIF, Local Program Improvement Fund. The BDUs still paid, contributing to the fund, which was split amongst local stations. But it was only for three years and diminished every year. Once it's gone, it's gone. And now it's gone, with no long-term solution in sight.

Actually, the regulator claims it has a solution—at least, it might have, based on the public input carried over for months during the "Let's Talk TV" hearings, as the CRTC asked "average Canadians" what they wanted on television.

One of the anticipated changes is to allow local stations to abandon their OTA (over-the-air) transmitters. They are enormously expensive, and it simply doesn't make sense to pay the cost of converting them to HD (high definition), as has been mandated. Surveys suggest less than 3 percent of Canadian viewers, at best, watch OTA television signals. It doesn't make sense for networks to upgrade, or even maintain, their system of transmitters in today's digital environment. If they didn't, almost no one would notice; the next generation of viewers (and an ever-growing number right now) would rather download what they want, when they want it, and usually on a mobile device.

In early 2015, the CRTC announced one of the first major policy changes to roll out after the "Let's Talk TV" hearings. There was speculation the transmitter announcement was coming. Instead, CRTC Chairman Jean Pierre Blais told reporters the commission was eliminating simultaneous substitution on Canadian re-broadcast of the Super Bowl Game, starting in 2017. What?

Simsub, as it is known in the industry, is the mandated system under which the signal from a Canadian broadcaster, which is simultaneously airing a US program to which it has purchased Canadian rights, must override the originated American channel that is carrying the same show. Basically, it means that if you're watching *Survivor*, you'll see the ads on Global even if you're watching a CBS station from the US.

It can be annoying, if the cable company forgets to make the switch cleanly after a program, or cuts out as a game is going into overtime. But for the most part, it works. And it's a good system to help Canadian broadcasters in the face of the overwhelming volume of American programming. And make no mistake, Canadians like watching American shows. I'm a big fan of locally produced entertainment shows, but there is a reason the list of hits is relatively short. Many Canadians just don't watch them.

Which brings us back to the Super Bowl. So, this is the CRTC's big announcement, its top priority? A decision that will cost a Canadian media company (in this case, CTV and ultimately Bell Media) millions of dollars and provide no benefit to the Canadian economy. And what is the reason? People apparently convinced the CRTC that we'd really like to see those funny US ads that debut during the game.

The decision also shows just how out of touch the CRTC really is. Does it not realize that digital media have overtaken the Super Bowl ad phenomenon? This year, the companies that forked over millions of dollars for a thirty-second spot made sure that it was released online first, in time to go viral before the game, so there was enough of a buzz for it not to slip by unnoticed in the third quarter. Companies released ads online they knew were not likely to even get on the air.

There was a time when Canadians felt deprived by the signal overcut that wiped out the American advertising showcase. But that day is long gone, and by 2017, who knows how it will play out. This cannot have been the commission's most pressing priority. As Canadian conventional television is gasping for breath, the CRTC seems to be reaching for that pillow.

The commission has since issued other new directives, including removing the mandate for Canadian content broadcast on television during the day. Critics warn this will ultimately result in less local news. CRTC policies have helped to kill small-market TV already. Just ask the people who used to work at RDTV in Red Deer, or CKX in Brandon, or my old alma mater, CHEK TV in Victoria.

What happened at CHEK is a great story of people who weren't willing to roll over and die. When Global couldn't find a buyer and was ready to turn out the lights and board up the windows, staff rallied and found a way to keep the station alive, buying it themselves. But for them, and not just them, Jim Morrison was right. The future's uncertain and the end is always near.

CHEK is in a struggle to survive, and it's not alone. It is doing better now but on a razor-thin margin, and thanks to the help of a different small-market program fund that was never really intended for that purpose. The commission made an exception, allowing CHEK to tap into it. Why? Because if stations like CHEK, or CHCH in Hamilton, are allowed to die, it will be proof that the CRTC's policies have failed.

But if the rules don't change, there will be others. Bell

Media, for example, has committed to its CTV Two stations only for a three-year period, and those licences will soon come up for renewal. You can only lose money for so long before you go out of business or shareholders demand change.

Bell Media's Kevin Crull told a 2015 TV conference in Ottawa that his company believes the CRTC should eliminate access to US network television, whose programs, for the most part, have all been bought and aired by Canadian networks. That probably isn't going to happen, and Crull won't be around to see it, if it does.

Kevin Crull learned a hard lesson when his pique at the CRTC and its chairman Jean-Pierre Blais got the best of his better judgement. Crull was outraged at a CRTC decision allowing consumers to move to a pick-and-pay system of choosing channels from their cable or satellite company. He called CTV News President Wendy Freeman, demanding that Blais not appear again that day on any CTV or Bell Media newscast she oversaw. Freeman acquiesced, though Blais was later included on the flagship CTV National News. When word of his gag order got out, Crull was condemned in the court of public opinion, and in a stern rebuke from the CRTC chair. In two weeks he was gone, and parent company BCE followed up with new rules to prevent something like this from happening again. Lesson: you can fire everybody in the room, but you can't mess around with their journalism.

The thing about the Crull incident that is perhaps most damaging is that it lends credence to the misguided view that there is a sinister corporate plot to manage the news of the day, with marching orders each morning about what to cover and how. In all my years in the business, it didn't happen to me. But I was gone by the time Wendy Freeman sent out her note after meeting with Kevin Crull.

Even in this era of citizen journalism, there will always be a need for news organizations that reflect local communities and have earned local trust. We used to stew about the five-hundred-channel universe. That seems quaint now. Our role as gate-keepers of the news is long gone. Anyone with a computer and a modem can broadcast or publish. Anyone with a smart phone, and that's just about everyone, can be a breaking news reporter at the scene of an event or disaster. And that's a good thing.

But the megaphone once enjoyed by only a few, and now available to most, carries responsibility. The words of Edward R. Murrow, in his seminal speech to the 1958 RTNDA convention in Chicago, the so-called "Wires and Lights in a Box" speech, still ring true: "It is not necessary to remind you of the fact that your voice, amplified to the degree where it reaches from one end of the country to the other, does not confer upon you greater wisdom than when your voice reached only from one end of the bar to the other."

The ubiquity of cameras uploading to social media sites can benefit the traditional newsgathering organs we have come to know and trust. But it also forces a collision of the ethics and mores that guided traditional versus what's acceptable or demanded by the new media.

The principles that guided the journalism of the past were largely developed from the rise of mass communication in the nineteenth century. Traditional journalistic values of accuracy, verification before dissemination, impartiality and gate-keeping have run head-on into the new culture and what it holds to be imperative: immediacy and transparency, a tilt in favour of the non-professional journalist and a willingness to accept corrections after the fact. Stephen Ward, founder of the Centre for Journalism Ethics at the University of Wisconsin, says the challenge is to create ethics and norms that cross all platforms of journalism, traditional or not.

Among the fundamental questions: what is journalism, and who is a journalist? And is it even relevant to a generation of Millennials, and those to come, for whom the old model seems archaic? At the end of the day, it boils down to trust. It doesn't matter whether you read something in an old-fashioned newspaper or on a website or a blog. Can you trust it to be true? Can we believe the people and organizations into which we have put our trust?

The remarkable thing about the story of Brian Williams and his suspension from NBC News in early 2015 is that it collided with the retirement of Jon Stewart from *The Daily Show*. Which was the bigger media story depended on who you talked to and how old they were. BuzzFeed's Steve Kandell perhaps summed it up best on Twitter: "A guy who reads the news is lambasted for making shit up at the exact moment a guy who makes shit up is lauded as a great newsman, what a world."

The sad thing, to me, about Brian Williams, whom I like, is what it has done to tarnish the credibility of everyone in broadcast journalism, whether on a network evening newscast, or a little station in Terrace or Medicine Hat. There is a widely held view that the so-called mainstream media cannot be trusted. And stories like this can only underscore that perception.

But all is not lost. Far from it. We have earned our credibility, but we must jealously guard it. And as we face uncertain times in conventional media, we must adapt and remember that change is the only constant. However, the method by which we deliver the news, regardless of how many are watching or listening or reading, there will always be the need for a trusted storyteller. Now, more than ever, just as it was learning more around the fire outside that cave with the painted walls.

# 20
# The Beginning

All of which brings us back to February 20, 2014, the morning I got the email from the station's general manager, inviting me to that meeting off-site. It was not the end. It was the beginning.

It has been more than a year now since we parted company, and I've learned a lot over the past several months. A lot about myself. As we go through life, especially if we choose a career like mine, we can get pretty heavily invested in "who we are." And we often confuse that with "what we do."

I have tried to never take myself too seriously, as many in our industry do. We can do good works and we can help people, but for the most part, we are not saving lives. And the fact that our face is on television, or our voice is on the radio, or our name and our thoughts are in print or online, does not confer any special status upon us.

I have enjoyed a remarkable career in this industry, taking me to heights I might never have imagined at the outset. And it isn't over yet. Losing my job when I did helped me put things into perspective. I have enjoyed the last year and it has opened my eyes. I have gone through life with a single-minded vision of what I wanted, and that's okay. But it kept me from using my peripheral vision to see all the other things that are out there. The blinders are off and I like what I see. I'm just getting started. Watch this space.

I have begun teaching at Royal Roads University. I have been writing. I have lost weight and am in better shape and, I hope, better health. Patty and I have been able to do some more travelling, and I now can commit more time to my home and family. I had never realized how long my workday was. I hadn't noticed. You don't, when you're doing what you enjoy.

Facing an uncertain future one year ago felt a little like that decision to jump out of a comfortable nest ten years earlier. It's like standing on the edge of a diving board. (I've never sky-dived or bungee jumped, or I'd use that analogy.) Don't be afraid. Make that leap. Don't look down. What's the worst thing that can happen? Don't let fear of failure keep you from taking a chance at succeeding. And don't let The Perfect be the enemy of The Good. Strive for imperfection—it could always be better. But always make sure you have a Plan B.

I have always said that we can all be taught pretty much every skill we need. But the two things that can't really be taught, that I always have looked for in people, are attitude and work ethic. Master those two things and there's nothing you can't do.

I have had some knocks and have suffered my share of loss, more than some, less than others. But it is in adversity that we discover and reveal our true character. I have been richly blessed in my lifetime, in more ways than I know. My family I love so much, my wife and our children. A comfortable living in the most beautiful city in the best province of the greatest country in the world. Dogs. Friends. Music. Travel. And, knock on wood, I have been able to enjoy it in good health. Be kind to others. Be good to yourself. And as Patty would say, "Enjoy!"

# Author's Note

By now you'd think that pretty much covers it. And it does. Except for a few final thoughts, some thank you's, and a little name dropping.

This book would not have been possible without the encouragement and support of my wife Patty. Nor would it have happened had it not been for the inspiration of my children, Hamilton, Sheldon and Rachel. As another Father's Day comes and goes I'm reminded again how very lucky I am to be their dad. And I can't help but wonder what my own father would think of all this. I often ponder what he'd make of the world today, so different from the one he left in 1974. A posthumous nod to him, my mother and sister and brother, and everyone in my life, the people I love and not just the ones I've lost, who helped make me who I am today. And to my extended family and friends who are so dear to me, thank you.

I'd be remiss in failing to thank the people who actually made this book a reality: my literary agent, Brian Wood (I never would've imagined saying I have one of those!) and everyone at

Harbour Publishing, especially my editor Derek Fairbridge, who cleaned up the copy, and made sense of my rambling recollections. Remember: Everyone's writing benefits from good editing.

Naming names is a mug's game, because invariably you leave out somebody you didn't mean to. But I can't help but mention a few, and a common thread for some of them is the old Broadcast News national newsroom at the Canadian Press in Toronto. It was there I made good and lifelong friends, Terry Scott and Keith Leslie, two of the best in the business and two of my favourite people. The RTDNA has introduced me to more people than I could list, and forged friendships to last a lifetime: Tom Mark and Gerry Phelan, Mike Stutz and Jon Stepanek, Eldon Duchscher and Mike Omelus (another BN alum). I've worked with, and for, many good and talented people in broadcasting: from reporters like Harry Maunu, sportscasters like Mira Laurence and technicians like Jason Noel (a veteran soldier I would follow into battle any day), to GM's who have encouraged me along the way, guys like Craig Roskin and Jim Blundell, and of course, Richard Gray and Brad Phillips who took me along on that amazing ride in 2001.

And if we're naming names, then I have to include a handful of nicknames too, because by now you can see I've given out more than a few. From The Duchess, The Stoker and Dr. Love, to Big D and The Big A (who still thinks it stands for Alex), Satan and The Iron Maiden, Citywide and QFC, Harv-Guard and Grider, Fonda Peters-Johnson, Willis and Sparky. They all know who they are.

One other name I have to mention is Hudson Mack. Not a reference in the dreaded third person, but Hudson Mack, the rock band. I discovered in the early to mid-1990s that an alternative Victoria band had chosen to use my name without permission. Their music could be described as post-punk hardcore, speed-rock, thrash-metal. I'm not sure any of those is an actual genre but you get the idea. They would dutifully drop off a copy of each new CD (and they released several), and I promised not to sue them until they made it big. They never really did, but in the early days of Google, if you searched for me the band would come up first, which I guess says something. They developed a large and loyal local following before finally splitting up. I always took their use of my name as a compliment, even if they were only inspired by the irony.

A few happenings to share from the past couple of months, as this tome was in its final stages. I have done some dabbling, toying with a return to the airwaves and coming close to taking the political plunge. The timing for each of them just didn't feel right, though I wouldn't rule out either one, eventually. We'll see.

My foray into the classroom has been a success, and I have new respect for teachers (not that I didn't have it already). Royal Roads University has invited me back and I expect I'll be there again, it's a great school and I am proud to be part of it. I was fortunate to expose my class to some top notch guest lecturers, among them media lawyer and friend Dan Burnett, and University of Victoria professor Dr. Janni Aragon. Janni's lecture and what happened afterward leads back to our story here, and reminds me again there are signs everywhere, if only you notice. Let me explain:

I had a thank you gift for her, a Royal Roads logoed scarf that I forgot to give the day she was in the classroom. I went to UVic to drop it off at her office but got lost. While asking for directions, I somehow ended up in the microfilm library. As I waited, I was browsing through neatly organized rows of microfiche, and noticed to my surprise that each box contained editions of the Calgary Herald through the 1950s and 60s. I knew there had been media coverage of Darrel's death in December 1956, and had some still unanswered questions with no one left to ask. I immediately found the box of microfilm containing that date, as if drawn to it. And as the librarian threaded the film into the viewer for me, the first image on the screen was the page containing the story of the shooting, the exact thing I was looking for. Someone, somewhere wanted me to see it.

I believe there are no coincidences. It's not by chance that I've been given the blessings and the challenges in my life, and it's no accident that you have chosen to let me share some of them with you. I'm glad I could. Thank you.

There is so much still to come, and I just can't wait.

PS: If you still haven't had enough, check out my RTDNA President's Award video at http://tinyurl.com/qbpnq4b. And stay in touch on Twitter with @HudsonHMack.

Cheers/HHM

# Index

Page numbers in **bold** refer to images

# Index